The Future of
Personal Information
Management
Part I: Our Information, Always and Forever

Synthesis Lectures on Information Concepts, Retrieval, and Services Editor

Gary Marchionini, *University of North Carolina, Chapel Hill*

Synthesis Lectures on Information Concepts, Retrieval, and Services is edited by Gary Marchionini of the University of North Carolina. The series will publish 50- to 100-page publications on topics pertaining to information science and applications of technology to information discovery, production, distribution, and management. The scope will largely follow the purview of premier information and computer science conferences, such as ASIST, ACM SIGIR, ACM/IEEE JCDL, and ACM CIKM. Potential topics include, but not are limited to: data models, indexing theory and algorithms, classification, information architecture, information economics, privacy and identity, scholarly communication, bibliometrics and webometrics, personal information management, human information behavior, digital libraries, archives and preservation, cultural informatics, information retrieval evaluation, data fusion, relevance feedback, recommendation systems, question answering, natural language processing for retrieval, text summarization, multimedia retrieval, multilingual retrieval, and exploratory search.

The Future of Personal Information Management, Part I: Our Information, Always and Forever

William Jones
2012

Search User Interface Design
Max L. Wilson
2011

Information Retrieval Evaluation
Donna Harman
2011

Knowledge Management (KM) Processes in Organizations:
Theoretical Foundations and Practice
Claire R. McInerney and Michael E. D. Koenig
2011

Search-Based Applications: At the Confluence of Search and
Database Technologies
Gregory Grefenstette and Laura Wilber
2010

Information Concepts: From Books to Cyberspace Identities
Gary Marchionini
2010

Estimating the Query Difficulty for Information Retrieval
David Carmel and Elad Yom-Tov
2010

iRODS Primer: Integrated Rule-Oriented Data System
Arcot Rajasekar, Reagan Moore, Chien-Yi Hou, Christopher A.
Lee, Richard Marciano, Antoine de Torcy, Michael Wan,
Wayne Schroeder, Sheau-Yen Chen, Lucas Gilbert, Paul
Tooby, and Bing Zhu
2010

2009

Introduction to Webometrics: Quantitative Web Research for the Social Sciences
Michael Thelwall
2009

Exploratory Search: Beyond the Query-Response Paradigm
Ryen W. White and Resa A. Roth
2009

New Concepts in Digital Reference
R. David Lankes
2009

Automated Metadata in Multimedia Information Systems: Creation, Refinement, Use in Surrogates, and Evaluation
Michael G. Christel
2009

The Future of Personal Information Management, Part I: Our Information, Always and Forever William Jones

ISBN: 978-3-031-01150-4 paperback
ISBN: 978-3-031-02278-4 ebook DOI 10.1007/978-3-031-02278-4

A Publication in the Springer series
SYNTHESIS LECTURES ON INFORMATION CONCEPTS, RETRIEVAL, AND SERVICES

Lecture #21
Series Editor: Gary Marchionini, University of North Carolina, Chapel Hill
Series ISSN
Synthesis Lectures on Information Concepts, Retrieval, and Services
Print 1947-945X Electronic 1947-9468

The Future of Personal Information Management

Part I: Our Information, Always and Forever

William Jones
University of Washington

*SYNTHESIS LECTURES ON INFORMATION CONCEPTS,
RETRIEVAL, AND SERVICES #21*

ABSTRACT

We are well into a second age of digital information. Our information is moving from the desktop to the laptop to the "palmtop" and up into an amorphous cloud on the Web. How can one manage both the challenges and opportunities of this new world of digital information? What does the future hold? This book provides an important update on the rapidly expanding field of personal information management (PIM).

Part I (Always and Forever) introduces the essentials of PIM. Information is personal for many reasons. It's the information on our hard drives we couldn't bear to lose. It's the information about us that we don't want to share. It's the distracting information demanding our attention even as we try to do something else. It's the information we don't know about but need to. Through PIM, we control personal information. We integrate information into our lives in useful ways. We make it "ours." With basics established, Part I proceeds to explore a critical interplay between personal information "always" at hand through mobile devices and "forever" on the Web. How does information stay "ours" in such a world?

Part II (Building Places of Our Own for Digital Information) will be available in the Summer of 2012, and will consist of the following chapters.

- Chapter 5. *Technologies to eliminate PIM?* We have seen astonishing advances in the technologies of information management—in particular, to aid in the storing, structuring and searching of information. These technologies will certainly change the way we do PIM; will they eliminate the need for PIM altogether?

- Chapter 6. *GIM and the social fabric of PIM.* We don't (and shouldn't) manage our information in isolation.

Group information management (GIM)—especially the kind practiced more informally in households and smaller project teams—goes hand in glove with good PIM.

- Chapter 7. *PIM by design.* Methodologies, principles, questions and considerations as we seek to understand PIM better and to build PIM into our tools, techniques and training.

- Chapter 8. *To each of us, our own.* Just as we must each be a student of our own practice of PIM, we must also be a designer of this practice. This concluding chapter looks at tips, traps and tradeoffs as we work to build a practice of PIM and "places" of our own for personal information.

KEYWORDS

PIM, personal information management, information overload, HCI, human-computer interaction, cognitive science, keeping found things found

This book is dedicated to Efthimis Efthimiadis whose smiling face I still expect to see as I go through the corridors of Mary Gates Hall. Efthi, your memory lives on.

Contents

Preface

All of my work, going back to my doctoral research into human memory long ago at Carnegie-Mellon University, has been motivated by the observation that information—at the right place and time, in the right form, and coherently organized—can help us to be very smart. Conversely, information missing or messy can overwhelm and make us stupid. How can we use information and information tools as an extension of ourselves and according to the lives we want to live?

Who should read this book? I wrote the book for the following audiences:

Faculty who are teaching PIM-related courses who can use the book both for a review of PIM basics and also to stimulate discussions concerning the future of our devices and the Web (Chapters 3 and 4).

People in PIM research who can use the book as an update on PIM-related research and perspectives.

People in related/contributing fields—including human-computer interaction (HCI), information retrieval (IR), library and information science (LIS), artificial intelligence (AI), database management, cognitive psychology and cognitive science – who can use the book as an efficient way to get up to speed on PIM.

People in business who want to know "what they should know" about PIM especially as it relates to employee productivity and the criteria for the selection of supporting tools. The book can't hope to be current with respect to supporting tools of PIM, but will provide guidelines for selecting PIM tools, techniques and policies.

Interested laypeople who want to know more about the field of PIM and who also hope to improve their own practices of PIM.

Some notes and caveats about this book:

- References to scholarly articles of direct relevance to personal information management (PIM) are grouped together into a bibliography at the end of the book (Part I). Web references and references for non-PIM background reading are generally included directly in footnotes.

- I include no references to information you can easily find on the Web. Instead of references, I sometimes include suggested search terms.

- I am an unabashed citer of Wikipedia (http://www.wikipedia.org/) articles when these are reasonably clear and objectively written. The interested reader should use these articles not as a final destination but as a springboard (through references cited) for further study of a given topic.

- The book is not a step-by-step "how to." It aims to help you in your efforts to figure things out for yourself.

- The book is not a review of the latest and greatest in PIM tools and technologies. Such a book is out of date even as it is being written.

- This book is no crystal ball. Instead, the book makes reasonable extrapolations from present trends into the future. Also, the book considers a "present perfect" of basic truths concerning our ways of processing information that have, are and likely always will, have relevance.

William Jones
March 2012

Acknowledgments

I thank Gary Marchionini for composing this lecture series.

I thank Diane Cerra for her assistance in getting this book to press.

I thank both Gary and Diane for their support and patience even as I repeatedly missed my (mostly self-imposed) deadlines.

I thank Abe Wenning for earlier research.

I thank my wife, Maria, for her comments on some portions of this book and for putting up with me as I struggled to complete this book.

William Jones
March 2012

CHAPTER 1

A New Age of Information

Information. We are overloaded and overwhelmed by it and yet we can't seem to get enough of it.

But what is information? This question has been a repeated topic of discussion[1]. Buckland, M. (1991), after an analysis of the many senses in which the word is used, concluded that "we are unable to say confidently of anything that it could not be information" (p. 256).

Indeed, the efforts people make to understand their world are usefully characterized as acts of information processing[2]. According to this view, our intelligence comes from our ability to process the raw data received through our senses into concepts, patterns, and implications. Everything "out there" that we are able to perceive is potential information.

Whether sensory data actually yields information depends. The seminal work of Shannon[3] introduced the notion that the information content of a message or event can be measured according to its impact on a recipient's current state of knowing (their level of "uncertainty"). The message that "Harry is coming to the meeting" has no information value, for example, if its intended recipient knows this already or if the message is given to the recipient in a language she does not understand. In neither case does the message change what she knows already concerning who will be attending the meeting.

But people don't exchange information just to reduce uncertainty[4]. Information, as the data of human communication, has a sender as well as a recipient. The sender may send the data to reduce the recipient's uncertainty (e.g., "It's raining out there, better take an umbrella"). But the sender may have other or additional intentions. The sender may want to impress or persuade or ingratiate. The sender may want to increase the recipient's uncertainty ("Have you considered these other possibilities ..."). The sender may even want to confuse or deceive. Likewise, the recipient may have aims other than to simply be "informed" by incoming data. The recipient may, for example, misconstrue the data to confirm or conform to pre-existing expectations.

In a survey of information science researchers described by Zins, C. (2007), information is often defined with reference to expressions of intention. For example, information is "the intentional composition of data by a sender with the goal of modifying the knowledge state of an interpreter or receiver" (p. 485). And information is "data arranged or interpreted ... to provide meaning" (p. 486).

A larger point in the work of Shannon endures: the value of information is not absolute but relative to a context that includes the intentions of the sender, the method of delivery, and the current state of a recipient's knowledge. The information value of data is in the eyes (ears, nose ...) of the beholder. What is information? We might better ask, what is information *to us*? Here are some answers.

Information is what we extract from the data of our senses in order to understand our world.

Information is what's in the documents, email messages, web pages, MP3 files, photographs (digital and paper-based), videos, etc., that we send (or post) and that we receive (or retrieve).

Information is for representing and referencing worlds distant from us in time or space. For example, information is how we learn about the ancient Egyptians. Information is how we learn of the current plight of people in a remote disaster area. Information is how we learn about the possibility of getting lung cancer in 20 years if we don't stop smoking.

Information is how we are represented to the outside world, accurately or not, for better or worse.

Information is a drain on our money, energy, attention and time.

Information is how we get things done.

Information is an extension of us.

Information is our challenge and our opportunity. We are bewildered, misled and seduced by information. But there is little we can do in our modern world that doesn't involve an exchange of information. Information, well managed, gives us a range and reach that far exceeds the limits of our physical selves. We can "see" to the ends of the earth and beyond. We can effect changes large and small: Provide a credit card number to reserve a hotel room; transfer ideas to transform lives.

Information is power.

What then is personal information? What makes it mine (or yours)? Look for the "me" in "mine." Information can be personal because it is "owned by me" (e.g., the information on our computer or on a flash drive), "about me" (e.g., medical records), "directed towards me" (think advertisements or dinner-time "marketing surveys"), "sent (posted) by me," "experienced by me" or, at the most general level, "relevant to me." Information in each of these senses is personal though for distinctly different reasons.

We gain from a management of personal information in each of these senses in accordance with the life we wish to lead. Likewise, we lose if personal information lays unmanaged or is managed by others in ways that work against us.

1.1 A DEFINITION OF PIM

Personal Information Management (PIM) refers to both the practice and study of the activities a person performs in order to locate or create, store, organize, maintain, modify, retrieve, use and distribute information in each of its many forms (in various paper forms, in electronic documents, in email messages, in conventional Web pages, in blogs, in wikis, etc.) as needed to meet life's many goals (everyday and long-term, work-related and not) and to fulfill life's many roles and responsibilities (as parent, spouse, friend, employee, member of community, etc.)[5].

The definition is broad and formal. But for our purposes, a more informal, working definition will often suffice. Mary Parker Follett, writing at the turn of the last century, defined management (of people) as "the art of getting things done through people."[6] Make a small substitution and we have: *PIM is the art of getting things done in our lives through information.*

PIM is not (just) about getting back to information we have experienced before, i.e., refinding, nor is it just about being better organized. We can think of people who are well organized—to a fault—but who appear no better able to manage either their information or their lives as a result. Conversely, we may know people who in their offices and their homes appear quite disorganized but who always *manage*, somehow, to stay on top of things.

We will review evidence from several sources to the point that organization does, in fact, matter. But not just any organization or organization for its own sake. Rather, organizing as a PIM activity should help us to make sense of and use our information. Organization should be towards one ideal of PIM: *to have the right information at the right time (and in the right form, of good quality, ...) to meet our needs*[7].

Or consider another ideal: Organizing information and other PIM activities are an integral and welcome part of our daily lives, not a separate chore to be guiltily postponed to "tomorrow." How might this be? Consider the screenshot in Figure 1.1 taken of a Web site for an amusement park in Sweden. Try it out (in a Web browser of your choice). The view in Figure 1.1 is animated. Cars and trains go back and forth. Carnival rides spin. Animals in the open air zoo move. Flags flap in the wind. Waves lap up against the beach. The water in the pool shimmers. Nothing fancy, but inviting and fun to look at, and functional. A click on the pool, for example, provides information concerning showers, changing rooms and places to eat nearby.

Can we imagine something similar as a kind of dashboard overview for our lives and our information? In the center might be a representation for home and family. Nearby might be representations for work and career, for health and fitness. Farther away there might be a snowcapped mountain or a beach to represent an interest in skiing or a vacation we hope to take. We might zoom in for greater focus on a specific area in our lives or a specific project.

The animation might change appearance to reflect important changes in our world. Clouds on the horizon might signal the imminent arrival of rainy weather; extra cars might represent a real traffic jam on our way to work. Items might change in color or increase in size to reflect looming deadlines.

Figure 1.1: Surely PIM is important but is it amusing?[8]

Such an animated "PIM dashboard" is certainly feasible even now and even more so as the computational power of our devices continues to improve. Whether the dashboard is merely a novelty or has enduring utility depends upon the nature of its implementation, the nature of our information needs and the nature of our natures as well.

A bigger point is that our visions of PIM should not be constrained by conventional images of a desktop or a file cabinet. Our informational overviews can be much richer and much more evocative. And a bigger point: PIM is not only necessary and important. It might even be fun.

1.2 WHO BENEFITS FROM BETTER PIM AND HOW?

PIM may be "personal" but better PIM promises to bring broad societal benefit.

Within organizations, better PIM means **better productivity** as employees develop a clearer understanding of their information needs and the ways in which tools and techniques of PIM can address these needs.

Such an understanding can also facilitate better teamwork and better group information management[9].

Progress in PIM is evidenced not only by better tools but also by teachable strategies of information management of direct relevance to education programs of information literacy[10].

People generally become more forgetful and their working memory span (the number of things they can keep in mind at one time) decreases with advancing age. Better PIM can translate to compensating tools and strategies of PIM to support our aging workforce and population.

The challenges of PIM are especially felt by people who are battling a life-threatening illness such as cancer even as they try, as nearly as possible, to live their lives and fulfill their roles as parent, spouse, friend and, even, as they try to maintain their jobs and profession-related activities. Better PIM can help patients manage better in their treatments and in their lives overall[11].

But certainly better PIM benefits people, regardless of their special circumstances. There is little chance you could be reading these lines were information and external forms of information (email messages, web pages, newspapers, this book) not of great importance to you in your everyday life.

Consider two kinds of people: *information warriors* and *information worriers*. Information warriors see their information and their information tools as a strategic asset. Information warriors are willing to invest time and money to keep up with the latest in mobile devices, tablet computers, smartphones, application software and anything new on the Web. For an information warrior, information technology is, so to speak, a profit center.

On the other hand, information technology for information worriers is a cost center. New offerings in mobile devices, new releases in operating system or application software, ...

new developments in the alphabet soup of Web-based initiatives—these and other developments in information technology represent more time and money that needs to be spent just to keep up with everyone else. Information worriers may have a nagging feeling they could do better in their choice of supporting tools and strategies. But they don't know where to begin.

Even if these descriptions are stereotyped, many of us can probably think of people we know who come close to each description. Perhaps you are an information warrior or an information worrier. Or perhaps you are a little of both.

For the simple fact is that even if we embrace new developments in information technology, we must recognize that we don't have time in the day to learn about all the latest developments. We need a basis for deciding whether a new tool or a new way of doing things is likely to work for us. We'd like to avoid an extended investment of money and, more important, time to learn the use of a new tool or strategy only then to conclude belatedly that it won't work for us.

Better PIM starts by asking the right questions. Better PIM means that each of us becomes a student of our practice of PIM.

1.3 RELATED FIELDS AND RELEVANT TERMS

PIM is a practical meeting ground for many disciplines including cognitive psychology/cognitive science, human-computer interaction (HCI), library and information science (LIS), artificial intelligence (AI), database management and information retrieval (IR).

People don't do smart things like PIM in isolation from an external environment that includes other people, available technology and organizational settings. Consequently, the study of *situated cognition, distributed cognition* and *social cognition*[12] all have relevance to the study of PIM. Also very relevant is the study of affordances provided by the environment and by the everyday objects of a person's environment[13]. People vary greatly in their approach to PIM-relevant behaviors such as planning and with respect to personality traits such as risk-aversion—making the study of individual differences and personality also very relevant to PIM[14].

1.3.1 A USEFUL INTERPLAY

Other fields contribute to PIM. PIM, in turn, provides a useful domain for the study in other fields. Benefits flow in both directions. The better, smarter searching methods that come from information retrieval (IR), for example, have obvious application to the finding and refinding of personal information. Similarly, as we learn more from the field of cognitive psychology concerning how information is represented in human memory, this understanding can guide us in our design of PIM tools to support in the keeping and organization of personal information. To take a simple example, what memories for an event in our lives (e.g., a party, vacation, wedding, graduation, etc.) will prove most durable over the long run—Time? Location? The people involved? The weather outside? Answers have direct implication to the design of a system for managing our photographs[15].

In the other direction, PIM offers many practical situations that might help to keep the researchers of other fields "relevant," so to speak, concerning the practical realities of everyday information management and use. For example, work on a big project such as "plan my wedding" can be viewed as an act of problem solving, and folders created to hold supporting information may sometimes resemble a problem *decomposition*[16]. For another example, the decision to keep or not to keep can be viewed as a *signal-detection task* and, as such, invites questions concerning the rationality of our keeping choices and our ability to estimate costs and outcome[17].

1.3.2 "PIMS" AND PDAS

PIM is often, incorrectly, equated with the development of "personal information managers" (some-times referred to as "PIMs") and personal digital assistants (PDAs)[18] which first appeared in the late 1980's and early 1990's. Characteristic of "PIMs" was the Sharp Wizard[19] first released in 1988 and famously featured on an episode of the TV show "*Seinfeld*"[20]. The Sharp Wizard was small enough to carry and offered an integrated set of basic functions for time and task management.

Today's handheld devices are much smaller and much, much richer in features and in raw computational power. But even as these devices solve some informational problems they create new ones. We can look up the location to a restaurant while we're driving … and we may very well kill ourselves and others if we try.

These days, the information we need may come from any of several sources—a hand-held device, a Web service as accessed from someone else's computer or, still, a paper-based source such as a print-out or a flyer. Also, PIM casts a broad net to include information of relevance to us for any of a number of reasons. We seek to manage, for example, not only "our" information but also the information *about* us or directed *towards* us.

1.3.3 HUMAN/COMPUTER INTERACTION, HUMAN-INFORMATION INTERACTION AND LIBRARY & INFORMATION SCIENCE

Much of the early PIM-related research came from practitioners in the field of *human-computer interaction (HCI)*. But concerns of PIM force us to look beyond the computer. PIM includes a consideration of our personal use of information in all of its various forms. Computer-based, for sure. But also paper-based. PIM brings an informational focus to everyday objects too. The light left on by the front door may be a reminder to take out the trash. The office door closed even though the light within is on may be sending our colleagues a message "I'm here but don't bother me unless it's really important."

In recent years, there has been discussion of *human-information interaction (HII)* in contrast to HCI[21]. In fact, arguments for a focus on information are not new. Fidel and Pejtersen (2004) asserted that the terms "human-information interaction" and "human information behavior (HIB)"represent essentially the same concept and can be used interchangeably. As such, HII-relevant discussions have been a long-standing mainstay in the field of library and information science (LIS) field[22].

People. Information. Tools (and technologies). Three concepts connected (see Figure 1.2). An initial focus on people and information (in the spirit of LIS, HIB & HII) eventually brings us to a consideration of the tools and technologies by which this information is created and stored, sent and received. An initial focus on people and tools eventually causes us to think about the information that is being managed (sent, received, created, stored) through the use of the tools under study. For example, we might study a person's use of a large-display device but without the broader perspective of PIM we might miss the sticky notes that encircle the display device.

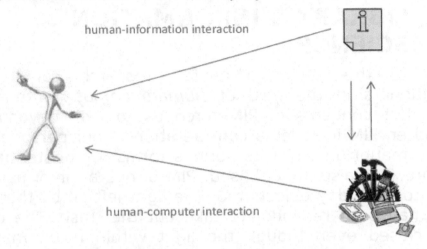
human-information interaction

human-computer interaction

Figure 1.2: The triangle of people, information and technology. A focus on the human-information interaction inevitably involves tools and technology (computer-based and otherwise). Likewise, a focus on the human-computer interaction inevitably involves a consideration of information.

1.3.4 KNOWLEDGE VS. INFORMATION, KNOWLEDGE MANAGEMENT VS. INFORMATION MANAGEMENT, PKM VS. PIM

The study of *information management* and *knowledge management* in organizations also has relevance to the study of PIM[23]. Issues seen first at an organizational level often migrate to the PIM domain. The merits of various schemes of classification or the use of controlled vocabularies, for example, have long been topics of discussion at the organizational level[24]. But these topics may find their way into the PIM domain, as the amounts of personally kept digital information continue to increase. This migration has already happened in the area of privacy, protection, and security[25].

Discussions often reflect an implicit ordering of the terms data, information and knowledge, i.e., information trumps data and knowledge trumps information. In a corporate/organizational context, information management came first as a field of inquiry, followed, beginning in the 1990s by discussions of knowledge management as a related but separate field of inquiry. Knowledge is, as O'Dell et al. said, "information in action" (1998, p. 5). Similarly, we might say that information is "data in motion"—data communicated, data sent or received with intention[26].

Now, predictably, we have discussions of personal knowledge management (PKM)[27], as a field of inquiry that relates to but is separate from personal information management (PIM). Elsewhere, I argue for the following[28].

1. Information is a thing to be handled and controlled; knowledge is not.

2. Knowledge can be managed only indirectly, through the management of information.

3. Personal knowledge management (PKM) is, therefore, best regarded as a subset of personal information management (PIM)—but a very useful subset addressing important issues that otherwise might be overlooked such as self-directed efforts of *knowledge elicitation* ("What do I know? What have I learned? How can I best communicate this knowledge the people I am training?") and *knowledge instillation* (i.e., "Learning what it is I need to know").

1.3.5 TIME, TASK AND PROJECT MANAGEMENT

The terms "task" and "project" (and associated terms such as "task analysis," "task management," "project management") mean different things to different people in different research communities[29]. Even within a single community such as the HCI community, the term "task" takes on different meanings in phrases such as "task management"[30] and "cognitive task analysis[31]. Also, "project" and "task" are often used interchangeably.

For PIM, a useful distinction is made between a *personal task* and a *personal project* or, simply, *task* and *project*. For *task*, we can use a simple, intuitive definition: A task is something we might put on a "to-do" list. "Pay bills," "Call mom to wish her a happy birthday," "Make hotel reservations" are all examples of tasks. With respect to everyday planning, tasks are atomic. A task such as "Make hotel reservations" can be decomposed into smaller actions —"Search for hotels in downtown area," "Select hotel," "Search for room," etc.—but there is little utility in doing so. A task can usually be completed in a single sitting but often stays on a to-do list of pending tasks for long periods awaiting the requisite information. We can't make hotel reservations, for example, until we know the dates of the trip and the location of the meeting.

A project, in turn, is made up of any number of tasks and sub-projects. Again, the informal "to-do" measure is useful: While it makes sense to put tasks like "Call the real estate broker" or "Call our financial planner" on a to-do list, it makes little sense to place a containing project like "Buy a new house" or "Plan for retirement" into the same list (except perhaps as an exhortation to "Get started"). A *project* has an internal structure of inter-dependent sub-projects and tasks and can last for weeks, months or even years.

Task management as used in recent studies of human-computer interaction[32] refers primarily to the management *between* tasks including handling interruptions, switching tasks and resuming an interrupted task. *Project management*, on the other hand, refers primarily to the management of various components *within* a project[33]. For the project to be successfully completed, many or most of these components must also be completed, in the right order, at the right time. In planning a family vacation, for example, it's important to make plane reservations but not before travel dates and destination are determined.

The informal task and project management that people perform as part of their everyday practice of PIM frequently differ from the more formal "industrial strength" task and project management [34], which is done (sometimes by managerial fiat) in an organizational setting and done also on occasion by highly disciplined individuals. People may use tools like the task module of Microsoft Outlook [35] or the web-based *remember the milk* [36] application for task management. But tasks are more commonly managed through more ad hoc methods, for example, "in our heads" or through notes scribbled on paper or through self-addressed email messages[37]. Projects too are frequently planned in our heads (e.g., as we're driving to work), or through notes quickly written to paper or an electronic document. Also, the folder structures people develop to hold project information can serve as a rough representation of project—its structure and current state of completion[38].

There is an important point that may already be obvious to many of you: task/project management and information management are two sides to the same coin. We manage (or should manage) our information with an end in mind— how will this information be needed and used later?[39] In some cases, a use is clear. We keep a slide presentation inside the "XYZ conference" folder because we'll be presenting the slides at the "XYZ conference." Folder organization in this case is a rough reflection of an anticipated reality. But this presentation may have other users later on that we don't foresee. The presentation may, for example, form the basis for another presentation we'll give later in the year at the "ABC conference." And for other kinds of information such as digital photographs, the use may be years, or decades, from now. Even so, we may file the photos according to features we think we're likely to remember, for instance by the year in which the photographs were taken or under a name for an associated event (e.g., "Sue's 50th birthday party").

Conversely, our efforts to plan a project or to prioritize and complete a set of daily tasks should also impact our management of related information. In fact, the structure of your project, with its various tasks and sub-projects, can form the basis for the organization of related information. A folder that implicitly represents the task to make "hotel reservations" can also contain information concerning hotel alternatives and a reservation confirmation for the hotel actually selected[40].

Two sides of the same coin. The same also holds true for our efforts to manage our life's resources—our money, energy, attention and—the only non-replaceable, non-renewable resource—our time. We can't effectively manage these without also managing associated information—our account and credit card statements and our calendars.

The PIM perspective gives us a stronger statement still: In a digital age of information, the very management of our tasks, our projects, our money, energy, attention and time are exercises in information management. We "see" our future by looking at the calendar(s) we keep. We feel richer or poorer after looking (on-line) at our checking account balances or the current prices of the stocks we hold. As we do so, we are not looking at and working with the "things" directly. Instead, we are looking at and working with information for these things.

1.4 A SHORT HISTORY OF PIM

Here is a newspaper-style history of PIM.

Ancient times. *Great new device released called the "human brain." Everyone gets one for free but without an owner's manual. Enormous capacity for storage but input and output can be especially difficult. Development of mnemonic techniques is underway but essential rhyming pattern awaits the invention of buns and shoes.*

The ultimate device of PIM was and still is the human brain—with capacities of associative storage and retrieval far exceeding that of our devices—current and conceivable. Various mnemonics[41] are essentially information management as applied to human memory.

Since ancient times, human-generated information has taken various external forms from cave drawings to clay tablets to parchment and papyrus to paper. For each form have come tools for writing, storage and retrieval. Tools need to be invented. Consider the vertical filing cabinet—around as long as any of us can remember but invented nevertheless[42].

The 1940s: *Information is a thing to be captured and measured!*

A theory of communication is developed which lays the groundwork for a quantitative assessment of information[43]. Information can be measured for its capacity to reduce uncertainty. The modern dialog on PIM begins with the publication of Vannevar Bush's "As we may think" article at the close of World War II (1945). Bush proposed a fanciful "Memex" as *"an enlarged intimate supplement to (a person's) memory"* (p. 6).

The 1950s: *The computer moves from metaphor to modeler of human thought.*

Newell and Simon pioneer the computer's use as a tool to model human thought[44]. Inspired by a computational metaphor, Broadbent develops an *information processing approach* to human behavior and performance (1958).

The 1960s. *Mind trips through hypertext, intelligence augmentation and human cognition.*

After the 1950s research showed that the computer, as a symbol processor, could "think" (to varying degrees of fidelity) like people do, the 1960s saw an increasing interest in the use of the computer to help people to think better and to process information more effectively. Working with Andries van Dam and others, Ted Nelson, who coined the word "hypertext," was part of a team that developed one of the first hypertext systems, The Hypertext Editing System, in 1968[45]. That same year, Douglas Engelbart also completed work on a hypertext system called NLS. Engelbart advanced the notion that the computer could be used to augment the human intellect[46]. In a similar vein, Licklider discussed the potential for a "Man-Machine Symbiosis" (1960). As heralded by the publication of Ulric Neisser's book *Cognitive Psychology* (1967), the 1960s also saw the emergence of cognitive psychology as a discipline in its own right—one focused primarily on a better understanding of the human ability to think, learn and remember.

1970s & 1980s. *A phrase is born.*

The personal computer comes into its own[47]. The phrase "personal information management" is coined[48] amidst a general excitement over the potential of the personal computer to greatly enhance the human ability to process and manage information. The 1980s also saw the advent of so-called "PIM tools" that provided limited support for the management of such things as appointments and scheduling, to-do lists, phone numbers, and addresses. And a community dedicated to the study and improvement of human-computer interaction also emerged in the 1980s[49].

1990s & 2000s. *A field is born*.

The Web is developed[50]. And so in succession are cell phones, personal digital assistants (PDAs), "smartphones" and integrative handheld devices that can seemingly do everything (except, it sometimes seems, establish a clear telephone connection)[51]. The process of building a community for the study of PIM began with a Special Interest Group session on personal information management, which was organized as part of the CHI 2004 conference on human-computer interaction[52]. But perhaps the watershed event in the creation of a PIM community was PIM 2005—a special NSF-sponsored workshop[53] held in January of 2005 in Seattle[54]. The participants formed a nexus for follow-on workshops[55], special issues[56] and an edited book on PIM[57].

1.5 A NEOLITHIC REVOLUTION IN PERSONAL INFORMATION MANAGEMENT

PIM is undergoing profound change. In our efforts to understand and track this change, we search for historical metaphors. This search takes us back in time—farther back than the 1940's and the dawning of the digital age—all the way back to the Stone Age.

Our ancestors were foragers. Before and even when they could hunt, our ancestors gathered and they scavenged the kills left by other animals. Application of the foraging metaphor has led to the development of information foraging models of PIM[58]: These models align our PIM activities with the food gathering activities of our ancestors during the Paleolithic age (early Stone Age). Under foraging models, we move from place to place across our informational landscape in ways that maximize the value of the information we expect to receive.

The Neolithic Age[59] (new Stone Age) followed the Paleolithic Age and farming followed foraging. Food foraged in the Paleolithic Age was farmed instead in the Neolithic age. Animals once hunted were domesticated and herded[60].

What about information farming? Will we "farm" information[61] rather than forage for it? And is the foraging model apt to begin with? Underlying both a foraging and a farming metaphor for PIM is a metaphor of information as food.

Is the metaphor of information as food apt?

There are interesting parallels to consider between food and information. Are we getting a "balanced" diet of information or too much informational sugar and fat in the form of, for example, of gossip magazines, celebrity tweets and news shows that treat political debates as sporting contests? Are we becoming informationally obese? We generally know little about the providers of the information we "consume." Do we need regulatory assurances for the quality of our information—comparable to those we expect for the food we eat?

These and other parallels notwithstanding, there are also important differences between information and food. Our bodies require certain essential vitamins and minerals but these can come from a variety of different foods. Vitamin C can come from a grapefruit or a freshly killed seal. Our bodies are adept at converting food from one form to another—from fat to sugars for energy now or, conversely, from carbohydrates to the fat of adipose tissue for use later on. Information is not a stuff to be so easily converted. Once informed that the stock markets closed lower today, we may make the inference that a stock we own is also trading lower. But such a "conversion" is neither straightforward nor assured. Farther afield, knowledge of the markets does not convert to a forecast for tomorrow's trading or for the weekend weather.

On the other hand, we can do with information what we cannot do with food: We can eat our informational cake and still have it. We do this, for example, when we watch re-runs of a favorite show on TV or listen for the nth time to a favorite piece of music or when we view again, with equal pleasure, the photographs we took during a summer vacation. Moreover, information consumed by us is still available for consumption by others. We can forward our photos.

Metaphors of information foraging and information farming may do more to challenge our creative abilities than to illuminate the challenges we face in managing our information.

For example, we "forage" for information in ways that build upon the information we have acquired already. This would seem to be quite unlike the foraging our ancestors did for berries. Facing a long, cold winter, we might always act to maximize the number of berries we gather. Facing a trip to Boston, our informational foraging quickly changes focus as a function of task: decide on dates of travel; book plane tickets; book hotel; make appointments and dinner reservations. Each task demands its own distinct kind of information. With task completion, the associated "informational berries" quickly lose their value. Once hotel reservations have been made, for example, there is little point to a continued gathering of information concerning alternate hotels[62].

Likewise, there are oddities with the application of a farming metaphor. We may think of situations where the metaphor is apt. We plant the "seed" of a blog post, for example, to grow a "vine" in the form of responses from others. But, more often, the metaphor seems strained. How do we sow our informational seeds? How is the field watered, fertilized and weeded? Is there a growing season? Are we informationally poor for the months of the growing season only to feast on an autumnal harvest? To be sure, we store information. But is this done to stave off an informational famine? Do we ration our information during the long months of winter?

Again, we can find answers to these questions. But these answers are more a testament to our creativity than to the aptness or utility of the foraging and farming metaphors. Exercises in the mapping of these metaphors do little to advance our understanding for the challenges of PIM.

In what sense, then, might we be facing a Neolithic Revolution in personal information? The original Neolithic Revolution brought about two profound changes in the way people lived and in their relationship to the world about them.

1. People actively worked not just to live in their environment but to change it.

2. People settled down.

Efforts to change the environment likely began in the Paleolithic Age with, for example, a seasonal firing of the prairie grasses to promote new growth in edible grasses and a return of game to feed on this growth[63]. But a transition to farming required a much greater, more local, and more focused concentration of efforts to control the environment. #2 above followed from #1. Ground must be tilled and fenced in to protect against the predations of animals, wild and domesticated. Granaries must be built to store the harvest. Walls must be built to protect against attack from neighboring nomadic tribes. Sedentism is self-reinforcing. It now makes sense to invest greater effort in permanent structures of habitation. Tools no longer need to be portable. Pottery, a heavy, non-portable kind of tool, is developed uniformly and independently across Neolithic cultures isolated from one another in time and space[64].

The parallels for personal information are approximate but intriguing. We have long been told that we live in an "information age." In a developed country like the United States, the onset of this age is sometimes traced back to a time in the 1950s when the number of white collar jobs exceeded the number of farming and blue collar jobs[65]. But we could extend backwards in time to a point where literacy, as promoted by public education, became widespread. We might well go farther back in time to the invention of the printing press and a resulting widespread availability of printed material in the form of newspapers, pamphlets and books.

Our understanding of our world is shaped not only by direct experience but also, indirectly, through the information we receive from books, billboards, magazines, newspapers, radio, TV and, of course, the Web. As Whittaker, S. (2011) notes we don't simply consume, we also curate, that is, we keep and manage information for later use. When print media dominated, for example, people saved clippings from newspapers and magazines. Many of us still do.

Living in an information age has personal relevance if we reflect upon the extent to which our interactions with our world are one step removed from direct experience and mediated, instead, through information items. In deciding to take an umbrella with us to work, we may check the Web for a forecast even before we look outside. In the other direction, many of the actions we take to effect change in our world (e.g., reserving a hotel room or delivering flowers for a friend in the hospital) are accomplished through an exchange of information items such as Web forms and emails.

Are we entering a new "Neolithic" age of information? What would it mean to "settle down" in a digital space of information? The pioneers among us have already long had settlements on the Web in the form of personal (or "professional") web sites. The rest of us are catching up. We may have one or several personal and professional web sites. We have Facebook[66] accounts and LinkedIn[67] accounts. We may even post our autobiographies to Wikipedia[68]. We can construct buildings or whole islands in Second Life[69]. A complete list of possibilities for the "settlement" of the Web gets longer with each passing moment.

And this is just the beginning. As we shall explore in the coming chapters, we can readily mold our digitally encoded information environment through a proliferation of tools— some of our own construction, many more crafted by others but available cheaply or for "free."

Settling down on the Web in this manner need not mean a concomitant "settling down" in our physical world. To the contrary, many of us may already feel a greater freedom to travel with assurances that we can keep in touch through email, text messaging, tweeting and voice-over-IP (VOIP). A permanent locatable presence on the Web may engender additional freedoms of movement in our physical world. We can post changes of physical and email address. Our web presence may "speak" for us in many routine situations— keeping a boss notified of changes in project status, for example, or keeping family and friends informed of our progress on a trip. We can grant controlled, qualified access to our calendars. We can even, if we choose, "tweet" our movements minute by minute. There is a real possibility that, through our devices and our Web settlements, our information can function as a kind of alter ego—the Enkidu to our Gilgamesh[70]—speaking for us, protecting us when we are otherwise occupied.

1.6 ROADS AND WALLS

Nomadic cultures still exist. A nomadic way of life thrives, for example, in large regions of Mongolia. Mongolian nomads are pastoralists—they tend their herds of cattle, yaks, sheep and goats. But they do not farm. Traveling through nomadic regions of Mongolia one is struck[71] by an absence of two structures so pervasive in an industrialized world: roads and walls. Travel through the Mongolian countryside is by jeep over open land and few roads are maintained outside of its towns. Likewise, outside of the towns in Mongolia, one sees few permanent vertical structures of any kind: no buildings, no walls, not even fences.

An informational settlement needs the metaphorical equivalent of both roads and walls[72]. "Roads"—in the form of search utilities and hyperlinks, for example, connect us to useful services and information (including the information in the settlements of others). Roads in the form of search engine optimization (SEO)[73] connect others to the services we want to provide and information we want to share.

"Walls" have a roughly opposite function. We may erect informational barriers (with varying degrees of effectiveness) in the form of "do not call" lists or the "disallow" of a robots.txt file. We use encryption, password-protection, and verification devices such as CAPTCHA[74]. We want to keep out the thieves, spammers and other unwanted intruders.

Informational walls are also a way to keep our information "in." Folders or tags, for example, if well-defined and consistently used, can provide a wall-like service in the partitioning of our information into useful groupings.

Without roads we stay ignorant and isolated. Without walls we are vulnerable to disorder, intrusion and attack. But both are a curse as well as a blessing. One main road—Internet connectivity—brings us to a world of information but also brings us phishing attempts ("Urgent: Please update your account ...") and hateful computer viruses that destroy our personal information. A wall in the form of junk email detection may block us from noticing an important email message. We may even find ourselves on the other side of a wall of our own construction—unable, for example, to open an encrypted file we've created because we can't recall the password.

No PIM construct is purely "road" or "wall" but, instead, a mixture of each. This is true whether the construct is a supporting tool or technique, a strategy or an overall system of organization. Throughout this book, we'll assess various constructs of PIM for their "road-like" and "wall-like" characteristics.

For starters, let's consider one of the most ordinary and widely used of PIM constructs: the file folder.

How is a folder like a road? How is it like a wall? For good and for bad? The folder's path is a kind of road (and aptly named as such). The folder's representation in a containing folder or on the computer desktop is road-like. When things go well, we see the folder's representation (e.g., a folder icon and the display of its name), recognize this as the folder that contains the information we seek and we open it to get at the desired information. By setting permissions for a folder we can realize a useful wall-like control over who can see and modify its contents. Also, folders keep our information grouped. Files and subfolders within move as the folder is moved. The grouping can be backed up or archived.

For the bad, we sometimes forget the way, take a wrong turn, and then fruitlessly look for the information we seek within the wrong folder. Or, we fail to recognize the folder even though it is "right there" in front of us. In these cases, the road is poorly marked and the folder is more like a bad wall—hiding its contents and keeping us on the "other side" of our information.

A recurring theme of this book is that, with the right tools and techniques of PIM, we can build roads and walls in our practice of PIM that work for rather than against us. Consider the fast, index-supported desktop search that is now standard on current operating systems. Evidence suggests that, at least for the return to documents and other files, people continue to prefer a road-like navigation through folders and subfolders[75]. However, on those occasions when navigation fails, people can now turn to search as an alternate "teleporting" method of return[76].

Furthermoe, consider the conventional file manager and its support for viewing and working with folder contents. The traditional model is perhaps too "wall-like" in the implementation of its features for file manipulation. We cannot easily see the contents of several folders at the same time. More recently, however, we now see support for "libraries"[77] and a outliner-like "in-place expansion" of folder shortcuts[78] as tool support that lets us break down the "walls" between folders In cases where we want to see a larger view of our information.

1.7 THE PLAN FOR THE REMAINDER OF THE BOOK

The remaining chapters in Part I ("The Future of Personal Information Management, Part 1: Our Information, Always and Forever") are as follows.

Chapter 2. Some basics of PIM. How is our information personal? The six senses in which information is personal combine to form a personal space of information (PSI). How do we manage our information? PIM as the creation, maintenance and use of a mapping between need and information yields six basic activities of PIM. PIM is about minute-by-minute tactical decisions of keeping and finding. PIM also needs to be about longer-term meta-level strategies for maintaining, organizing, measuring and making sense of personal information.

Chapter 3. Our information, always at hand. How do we manage when a device that fits in the palm of a hand affords access to a world of people and information that is by turns useful, entertaining, distracting and demanding? Through mobile devices, our physical and digital worlds meet—and sometimes collide. We're always connected but always on call. How to avoid the dangers of multitasking "busyness." How to really get "real" things done and, in the process, how to preserve precious memories for a lifetime and beyond?

Chapter 4. Our information, forever on the Web[79]. We must learn to live with, through and "on" the Web. Many of us look for ways to move from scattered "nomadic camps" on the Web to consolidated, permanent settlements where our investments in the management of our information pay off. We need help from our applications. How to transition from vertical, monolithic, "do everything" applications that fragment to horizontal, PIM-activity-centered applications that work together towards a common unity of personal information?

Chapters in Part II ("The Future of Personal Information Management, Part 2: Building Places of Our Own for Digital Information") are as follows.

Chapter 5. *Technologies to eliminate PIM?* We have seen astonishing advances in the technologies of information management—in particular to aid in the storing, searching and structuring of information. These technologies will certainly change the way we do PIM; will they eliminate the need for PIM altogether?

Chapter 6. *GIM and the social fabric of PIM.* We don't (and shouldn't) manage our information in isolation. Group information management (GIM), especially the kind practiced more informally in households and smaller project teams, goes hand in glove with good PIM.

Chapter 7. *PIM by design.* What are some of the methodologies, principles, questions and considerations we can apply as we seek to understand PIM better and to build PIM into our tools, techniques and training?

Chapter 8. *To each of us, our own.* Just as we must each be a student of our own practice of PIM, we must also be a designer of this practice. This concluding chapter looks at tips, traps and tradeoffs as we work to build a practice of PIM and "places" of our own for personal information.

Some final notes and caveats:

References to scholarly articles of direct relevance to PIM are grouped together into bibliographies at the end of both Parts I and II. Web references and non-PIM references for background reading are generally included directly in footnotes.

I am an unabashed citer of Wikipedia (http://www.wikipedia.org/) articles when these are reasonably clear and objectively written. The interested reader should use these articles not as a final destination but as a springboard (through references cited) for further study of a given topic.

Although each chapter builds upon previous chapters, each stands on its own. You do not need to read in sequence. But do try to read the next chapter, "Some basics of PIM," before reading the others.

The book is not a step-by-step "how to." It aims to help you in your efforts to figure out things for yourself.

The book is not a review of the latest and greatest in PIM tools and technologies. Such a book is out of date even as it is being written.

This book is no crystal ball. How then, is this a book about the "future" of PIM? In two ways:

The book makes reasonable extrapolations from present trends into the future.

The book considers a "present perfect" of basic truths concerning our ways of processing information that have, are and likely always will have relevance.

Present trends and a present prefect of enduring truths: With these clearly in focus, may we each be empowered to determine our own future. May we each lead the lives we wish to live through the artful use of information.

[1] For general discussions concerning information and its definition see Braman, S. (1989), Buckland, M. (1991, 1997), Capurro and Hjørland (2003), Cornelius, I. (2002), Machlup, F. (1983).

[2] See, for example, Broadbent's "Perception and communication" Broadbent, D. (1958) for a discussion of the information processing approach to understanding human intelligence.

[3] See Shannon, C. (1948) and Shannon and Weaver (1949) for a description of "The Mathematical Theory of Communication."

[4] For "post-Shannon" views of what information is and how it might be measured see Aftab et al. (2001), Capurro and Hjørland (2003) and Cornelius, I. (2002).

[5] This definition of PIM is taken from Jones, W. (2007).

[6] Daft, Richard L, 1988, Management, p. 5, Dryden Press, ISBN-13: 9780030094736 ISBN: 0030094739.

[7] Jones and Maier (2003).

[8] The screenshot is taken of the web site for Furuvik in Sweden (http://www.furuvik.se/#1041).

[9] For more on group information management, see Lutters et al. (2007).

[10] For a review of information literacy initiatives see Eisenberg et al. (2004).

[11] Pratt et al. (2006).

[12] See, for example, Fiske, and Taylor (1991); Hutchins (1994); and Suchman (1987).

[13] The interested reader is referred to Gibson's groundbreaking work on affordances (1977, 1979). Also very interesting and more accessible are Norman's discussions on the impact that "everyday things"—computer based and not—can have on our ability to handle information (1988, 1990, 1993).

[14] For a discussion of individual differences as these apply to PIM, see Gwizdka and Chignell (2007). (See also Boardman and Sasse (2004), Malone, T. (1983), Whittaker and Sidner (1996).)

[15] For a fascinating study of how (how well) people retrieve photographs they have taken, see Whittaker et al. (2010).

[16] See, for example, Jones et al. (2005).

[17] The signal-detection analysis was originally developed by Peterson et al. (1954). For its application to keeping decisions see Jones, W. (2004). For a more general discussion on the interplay between cognitive psychology and PIM, see Jones and Ross (2006).

[18]See http://en.wikipedia.org/wiki/Personal_information_manager, http://en.wikipedia.org/wiki/Category:Personal_digital_assistants, http://en.wikipedia.org/wiki/List_of_personal_information_managers.

[19]http://en.wikipedia.org/wiki/Sharp_Wizard.

[20]http://en.wikipedia.org/wiki/Seinfeld.

[21]See, for example, Fidel and Pejtersen (2004), Gershon (1995), Lucas (2000) and Pirolli (2006).

[22]See, for example, Belkin et al. (1993).

[23]For more discussion on information management and knowledge management in organizations, see Garvin (2000), Selamat and Choudrie (2004), Taylor (2004) and Thompson et al. (1999).

[24]See, for example, Fonseca and Martin (2004) and Rowley (1994).

[25]See, for example, Karat et al. (2006).

[26]Why stop with knowledge? Factoring in "wisdom" we might have the following sequence: Information is data in motion; knowledge is information in action; wisdom is knowledge in perspective.

[27]Pauleen D. and Gorman G., Farnham Personal Knowledge Management: Individual, Organisational and Social Perspectives, in: Gower Pub Co. Retrieved from http://www.gowerpublishing.com/default.aspx?page=641&calcTitle=1&isbn=9780566088926&lang=cy-GB

[28]http://firstmonday.org/htbin/cgiwrap/bin/ojs/index.php/fm/article/view/3062/2600.

[29]Grudin, J. (1993).

[30]See Bellotti et al., 2004; Bellotti et al. 2003; Czerwinski et al. 2004; Gwizdka, 2002 a, b; Kaptelinin, 2003; Kim and Allen, 2002; Mackay, 1988; Silverman, 1997; Whittaker and Sidner (1996); Williamson and Bronte-Stewart, 1996; Wolverton, 1999; Yiu, 1997.

[31]See Card et al. (1983).

[32]See Bellotti et al., 2003, 2004; Czerwinski et al., 2004; Gwizdka, 2002 a, b; Kaptelinin, 2003; Kim and Allen, 2002; Mackay, 1988; Silverman, 1997; Whittaker and Sidner (1996); Williamson and Bronte-Stewart, 1996; Wolverton, 1999; Yiu, 1997.

[33]See Jones, Bruce, & Foxley, 2006; Jones, Bruce, Foxley, & Munat, 2006; Jones, Munat, & Bruce, 2005; Jones et al. (2005).

[34]http://en.wikipedia.org/wiki/Task_management; http://en.wikipedia.org/wiki/Project_management.

[35]http://office.microsoft.com/en-us/outlook-help/create-tasks-and-to-do-items-HA001229302.aspx.

[36] http://www.rememberthemilk.com/

[37] Jones et al. (2002).

[38] See Bergman et al. (2010) and also Jones et al. (2005).

[39] Bruce, H. (2005)

[40] See Bergman et al. (2006). Boardman and Sasse (2004), Jones et al. (2005). The Planz prototype represents one approach that supports an informal project planning as an overlay to the file system (for free download, visit: http://kftf.ischool.washington.edu/planner_index.htm).

[41] For an excellent review of mnemonic techniques, see Yates, F. (1966).

[42] Yates, J. (1989).

[43] Shannon, C. (1948); Shannon and Weaver (1949).

[44] For a description of these pioneering efforts to model human thought, see Newell and Simon (1972), Newell et al. (1958), Simon and Newell (1958).

[45] For more on this early hypertext system and Nelson's impassioned discussion concerning the potential of hypertext, see Carmody et al. (1969) and Nelson, T. (1965, 1982).

[46] For more on NLS and a discussion on the potential of computers to extend the human capacity for thought, see Engelbart, D. (1962, 1963).

[47] http://en.wikipedia.org/wiki/Personal_computer.

[48] See Lansdale, M. (1988).

[49] See Card et al. (1983), Norman, D. (1988).

[50] http://en.wikipedia.org/wiki/World_Wide_Web.

[51] http://en.wikipedia.org/wiki/Personal_digital_assistant.

[52] See Bergman et al. (2004).

[53] National Science Foundation (NSF) grant #0435134: http://www.nsf.gov/awardsearch/showAward.do?AwardNumber=0435134.

[54] For more information on this PIM 2005 workshop and to access its final report, see: http://pim.ischool.washington.edu/pim05home.htm.

[55] As of this book's publication, the most recent of these PIM workshops was PIM 2012, held in association with CSCW 2012 back again in Seattle (http://pimworkshop.org/2012—see at the bottom of this site's home page for a listing of links to the 4 preceding PIM Workshops.

[56] The January 2006 issue of the *Communications of the ACM* included a special section on PIM (see Teevan, J., Jones, W., and Bederson, B. (eds.). *Communications of the ACM: A Special Issue on Personal Information Management*. New York: ACM Press, 2006). A special issue on PIM for *ACM Transactions on Information Systems* was released in 2008.

[57]See Jones and Teevan (2007).

[58]Pirolli and Card (1999)

[59]http://en.wikipedia.org/wiki/Neolithic;
http://en.wikipedia.org/wiki/Neolithic_Revolution.

[60]See: Bellwood, P. (2004). *First Farmers: The Origins of Agricultural Societies.* Blackwell Publishers. ISBN 0-631-20566-7. Cohen, M. N. (1977). *The Food Crisis in Prehistory: Overpopulation and the Origins of Agriculture.* New Haven and London: Yale University Press. ISBN 0-300-02016-3. Harlan, J. R. (1992). *Crops & Man: Views on Agricultural Origins* ASA, CSA, Madison, WI. http://www.hort.purdue.edu/newcrop/history/lecture03/r_3-1.html. Gordon Childe (1936). *Man Makes Himself.* Oxford University Press. Wright, R. (2004). *A Short History of Progress.* Anansi. ISBN 0-88784-706-40. Barker, G. *The Agricultural Revolution in Prehistory: Why did Foragers become Farmers?* OUP Oxford (Jan. 22, 2009) ISBN 978-0199559954 pp. 292–293.

[61]Bates, M. (2002) discusses an information farming model noting, for example, that people often assemble information into collections for later use (similar to our storage of food for later consumption).

[62]Whittaker, S. (2011) challenges the foraging model of information behavior and, more generally, consumption models of PIM. He advances, instead, a model in which we curate our information (keeping, managing and sometimes exploiting the information we encounter).

[63]See Wikipedia for an excellent article on the uses of prairie firing in North America (http://en.wikipedia.org/wiki/ Native_American_use_of_fire).

[64]Wikipedia provides an excellent starting point for learning more about the (often independent) development of pottery in different Neolithic cultures (http://en.wikipedia.org/wiki/Pottery).

[65]See Naisbitt's book (1984), "*Megatrends: Ten new directions transforming our lives.*" The reader is also invited to review for the accuracy (nearly 30 years ago) of this book's attempts to predict the future.

[66]www.facebook.com.

[67]http://www.linkedin.com/.

[68]http://www.wikipedia.org/.

[69]http://secondlife.com/.

[70]http://en.wikipedia.org/wiki/Gilgamesh.

[71]As I was during a trip made in the summer of 2003.

[72]As an exercise, the reader might try a broader application of the "road" and "wall" metaphors. Roads stand for flow, exchange and movement. Walls for stasis and the restriction of movement. Roads are for projection and an optimistic anticipation of gain (the pot of gold at the end of the rainbow); walls are for protection and a more pessimistic fear of loss. Activities of youth are

more road-like; activities of age are more wall-like. The Internet in its youth was very road-like. But now we are increasingly seeing efforts to build walls, for example, in the form of areas of restricted or privileged access. Farther afield, it is interesting to note the "road" and "wall" themes expressed in two "master plots" of literature: "The hero takes a journey" and "Stranger comes to town" (http://teachingcompany.12.forumer.com/a/9-master-plotsthe-stranger-and-the-journey_post2248.html).

[73]Wikipedia provides an excellent article on SEO (http://en.wikipedia.org/wiki/Search_engine_optimization). For a longer, highly readable treatment see on-line "The Beginner's Guide to SEO" (http://www.seomoz.org/beginners-guide-to-seo).

[74]http://en.wikipedia.org/wiki/CAPTCHA.

[75]Barreau, D. (2008); Bergman et al. (2008).

[76]Teevan et al. (2004).

[77]http://en.wikipedia.org/wiki/Windows_7.

[78]http://en.wikipedia.org/wiki/Planz.

[79]Technically speaking, the World Wide Web or, simply, the Web, is built using the Internet (see http://www.answers.com/topic/web-vs-internet). However, the terms are used interchangeably throughout this book.

CHAPTER 2

The Basics of PIM

In our practices of PIM, we are (or should be) in charge. In sentences describing our behavior, we're the subject. That's the "P" in PIM. The object of these sentences is information in one form or another—the "I" in PIM. And the verb is some PIM activity—the "M."

This chapter concerns basics of the "I" and the "M" of PIM. The first section, on the way to defining a space of personal information, considers what it means for information to be manageable and some of the "whys" for doing so. The second section considers basic activities of PIM and the mapping between information and need that is realized (implicitly) through these activities.

2.1 INFORMATION AS THE OBJECT OF PIM

In Chapter 1, Buckland is quoted as saying "we are unable to say confidently of anything that it could not be information"[79]. We can't manage it all. However, Buckland offers a useful slant on "information-as-thing" which fits nicely with the derivation of "management." The word comes from "manage" which derives from the Latin "*manus*"—hand[80]. PIM is focused on the information we "touch" and manipulate—if not directly, as we do for paper-based forms of information, then at least indirectly through our information tools.

2.1.1 THE INFORMATION ITEM AND ITS FORM

Information-as-thing is something tangible to be manipulated—to be created, copied, stored, retrieved; given a name, tags, and other properties; and moved, copied, distributed, deleted, and otherwise transformed. In this spirit, it is useful to speak of an information item and its associated form:

An **information item** is a packaging of information. Examples of information items include: 1. paper documents, 2. electronic documents, digital photographs, digital music, digital film and other files, 3. email messages, 4. web pages or 5. references (e.g., shortcuts, aliases) to any of the above. Items encapsulate information in persistent forms that can be created, modified, stored, retrieved, given a name, tags and other properties, moved, copied, distributed, deleted and otherwise manipulated.

For a information item it is often useful to speak of an associated **information form** which is determined by the tools and applications that support the operations listed above. Common forms of information include paper documents, e-documents and other files, email messages and web bookmarks[81].

The ways in which an item is manipulated will vary depending on its form and the tools available for this form. The tools used for interaction with paper-based information items include, for example, paper clips, staplers, filing cabinets, and the flat surfaces of a desktop. In interactions with digital information items, we depend on the support of various computer-based tools and applications such as email applications, file managers, and web browsers. The ways we delete a paper document differ from the ways we delete an electronic document (e.g., tossing in the trash or shredding vs. using the commands "cut" or "delete"), but some notion of deleting applies to each (a similarity the Macintosh reinforces through its metaphorical "trash can").

This book will use "information item" in preference to "document" when generally describing the information we wish to manipulate and better manage through our practices of PIM. However, in a Web-based world where pages of information can be stitched together on demand, we must allow for the possibility that the actual bits of an item may change with each viewing. It is often useful, therefore, to discuss an item with reference to its address. We will speak of folder paths (e.g., UNC paths) to files, URLs for web pages and, more generally, URIs[82] as a means to address information items and other things too (e.g., physical objects like keys or chairs and even people). A URI "de-referenced" returns an information item.

2.1.2 HOW IS INFORMATION PERSONAL?

Why bother to manage information (even if we can)? We're motivated to manage because information matters to us, personally, in one way or another. Think of the possible connections between "information" and "me." As summarized in Table 2.1[83], information can be owned by me; about me; directed towards me; sent or published by me; experienced by me or, "relevant to" me. Each kind of personal information is briefly described below.

1. **Controlled by (owned by) me.** The information a person keeps, directly or indirectly (e.g., via software applications),for personal use is personal information. Included are e-mail messages in an e-mail account, files on the hard drive of a personal computer and also the paper documents kept on surfaces and inside conventional filing cabinets[84].

Table 2.1: The senses in which information can be personal.

	Relation to "me"	Examples	Issues
1	Controlled by, owned by me	E-mail messages in our e-mail accounts; files on our computer's hard drive.	Security against break-ins or theft, backups, virus protection, etc.
2	About me	Histories of credit, medical, Web browsing, library books checked out, etc.	Who sees what when (under which circumstances)? How is information corrected or updated? Does it ever go away?
3	Directed towards me	Phone calls, drop-ins, TV ads, Web ads, pop-ups.	Protection of me and my money, energy, attention and time.
4	Sent (posted, provided) by me	E-mail, personal Web sites, published reports and articles.	Who sees what when? Did the message get through?
5	(Already) experienced by me	Web pages that remain on the Web. Books that remain in a library. TV and radio programs that remain somewhere in "broadcast ether."	How to get back to information again later?
6	Relevant (useful) to me	Somewhere "out there" is the perfect vacation, house, job, life-long mate. If only I could find the right information!	If only I knew (had some idea of) what I don't know. How to filter out or otherwise avoid information we don't wish to see? (How to do likewise for our children?)

2. **About me.** Information about a person but available to and possibly under the control of others is a second sense of personal information. Personal information in this category includes the information about a person kept by doctors and health organizations, for example, or the information kept by tax agencies and credit bureaus.

3. **Directed towards me.** Included in this category is the e-mail that arrives in the inbox and also the pop-up notifications that this new e-mail has arrived. Alerts raised by a person's computer, the "push" of advertisements on a visited Web page or the ringing

telephone are all examples of information directed towards a person. The information itself may or may not be personally relevant. But the sender's intention is personal and so too is the potential impact of the information on the person. Information directed to a person can distract the person from a current task, consume a person's attention and convince the person to spend time, spend money, change an opinion or otherwise take an action. We may be inclined to think of this incoming information as a nuisance, but sometimes this information serves the recipient well—a fire alarm in the case of a burning building, for example, can be a lifesaver.

4. **Sent (posted, provided) by me.** Information sent by the person (or posted, published) is a fourth kind of personal information. This information may or may not contain information about the person. But the person as sender is personally invested in seeing that the information gets to its intended recipients and has the intended effect. And perhaps the person is also invested in efforts to keep the information away from other people. For example, we may try to control, albeit imperfectly, who first sees the information in an e-mail message we send. We may try to do this through choice of distribution lists and by including notices on the e-mail messages such as "Confidential, please do not distribute."

5. **Experienced by me.** Information experienced by a person is also personal information. Some of this information is under the person's control and so also personal in the first sense of personal. Other information is not under the person's control: the book a person browses (but puts back) in a traditional library, for example, or the pages a person views on the Web.

6. **Relevant (useful) to me.** A final sense in which information can be personal is determined by whether this information relevant or useful to the person. Included is the information close at hand that we have assembled in order to understand a situation better or to make a decision. Also included is the information we don't have available and that we may not even know about but the we "ought" to know about. Out there, somewhere, is an article that is perfect for a report we're writing or an advertisement for a vacation package that perfectly fits our needs. Note that whether information is personal in this sixth sense of personal is greatly dependent upon a shifting context of need and current awareness. If I've forgotten about a meeting that I am expected to attend, then a reminder is very relevant. And then so too is information concerning the weather or traffic congestion en route. This same reminder is not relevant (and even an annoyance) if I know about and am already taking steps to attend the meeting. With respect to this expanded "sixth sense" of personal, we depend upon "filters"—in the form of tools, habits and our social networks—both to filter in the information we'd like to see and to filter out the information we do not want to see.

2.1.3 DEFINING A PERSONAL SPACE OF INFORMATION

When information in each of its senses is added together, each of us has a unique personal space of information, or PSI[85], as depicted in Figure 2.1. Our PSI is everything informational as it relates to us. We each have only one PSI. We inhabit this space as surely as we inhabit our physical space. And our informational space affects the way we experience and are experienced in our physical space.

A person's PSI might be visualized as a vast sea of personal information. If the "home waters" represent information under the person's control, then, farther out in the PSI, are waters of information that are shared, disputed or under exploration. This area includes information about the person, the use of which the person might like to control (or at least monitor) but which is currently under the control of others (credit agencies, tax authorities, insurance companies, etc.). At the periphery of a person's PSI are oceans of available information (on the Web, corporate intranets, public libraries, etc.), only the tiniest fractions of which the person explores in order to complete various tasks and projects and in order to fulfill various roles in the person's life.

Even in home waters of the PSI, a person's sense of control over information is partly illusory. For example, an email message can be deleted and no longer appear. However, the message is very likely still in existence. We're adrift in a sea of information. Our own personal spaces of information (PSI) are large, mostly unexplored, with uncertain boundaries and big areas of overlap (with the PSIs of other people and organizations).

But PIM is about extending our control, or at least our influence, out over this sea of personal information. We will never have perfect control. We do what we can. And most of us can do much more than we're doing now.

2.1.4 PERSONAL INFORMATION COLLECTIONS

Are there islands in this sea of personal information? Several researchers have discussed the importance of collections in managing personal information[87]. This book uses the definition of "personal information collections"(PICs) from Jones, W. (2007):

> *Personal information collections, referred to as " PICs" or simply " collections" in the remainder of the book, are personally managed subsets of a PSI. PICs are "islands" in a PSI where people have made some conscious effort to control both the information that goes in and how this information is organized.*

PICs can vary greatly with respect to the number, form, and content coherence of their items. Examples of a PIC include:

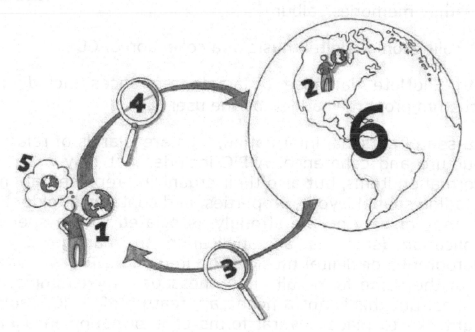

Figure 2.1: Six senses of personal information to make a personal space of information (PSI)[86].

The papers in a well-ordered office and their organization, including the layout of piles on a desktop and the folders in filing cabinets.

The organized papers in a specific filing cabinet and their organizing folders where, perhaps, the office as a whole is a mess.

Project-related information items that are initially dumped into a folder on our notebook computer and then organized over time.

A carefully maintained collection of bookmarks to useful reference sites on the Web and their organizing structures.

A collection of digital photographs and videos in a "family memories" album.

A collection of digital music or a collection of CDs.

An EndNote database of article references including custom properties added by the user[88].

In a sea of personal information, PICs are islands of relative structure and coherence. A PIC includes not only a set of information items, but also their organizing representations, including spatial layout, properties, and containing folders. A PIC may or may not be strongly associated with a specific application (such as an application to manage digital photographs or digital music). The items in a PIC will often be of the same form—all email messages, for example, or all files. But this is not a necessary feature of a PIC. People might like to place several forms of information in a PIC, even if doing so is often difficult or impossible with current software applications.

Just as the information item is self contained as a unit for storage and transmission of information, the PIC is self-contained with respect to the maintenance and organization of personal information. People typically refer to a PIC when they complete a sentence such as "I've got to get this [papers | email | photographs | documents] organized!" The organization of "everything" in a PSI is a daunting, impossible, task. But people can imagine organizing a collection of web bookmarks, their email inbox, their laptop filing system (at least in selected regions), and so on. Likewise, in the study of PIM, PICs are a tractable unit of analysis, whereas consideration of a person's entire PSI is not.

2.2 THE MANAGING ACTIVITIES OF PIM

PIM activities are an effort to establish, use, and maintain a mapping between information and need.

2.2.1 DEFINING A MAPPING

The simple statement above can be expanded, and PIM activities interrelated, with reference to the diagram in Figure 2.2. Needs[89], as depicted in the rightmost column, can be expressed in several different ways. The need may come from within a person as she recalls, for example, that she needs to make plane reservations for an upcoming trip. Or it may come via the question from a colleague in the hallway or a manager's request. Needs themselves are evoked by an information item such as an email message or a web-based form.

Information, as depicted in the leftmost column, is also expressed in various ways—as spoken comments from a friend or as a billboard seen on the way to work or via any number of information items including documents, email messages, web pages, and handwritten notes.

Connecting between need and information is a mapping. Only small portions of the mapping have an observable external representation. In a company or as individuals, for example, we maintain folder structure or a tagging scheme which is visible in our filing systems, digital and paper-based. However, much of a mapping has only hypothesized existence in the memories of individuals and perhaps also in the policies, procedures and daily workflows of an organization. Large portions of the mapping are potential and not realized in any form, external or internal. A sort function or a search facility, for example, has the potential to guide from a need to desired information.

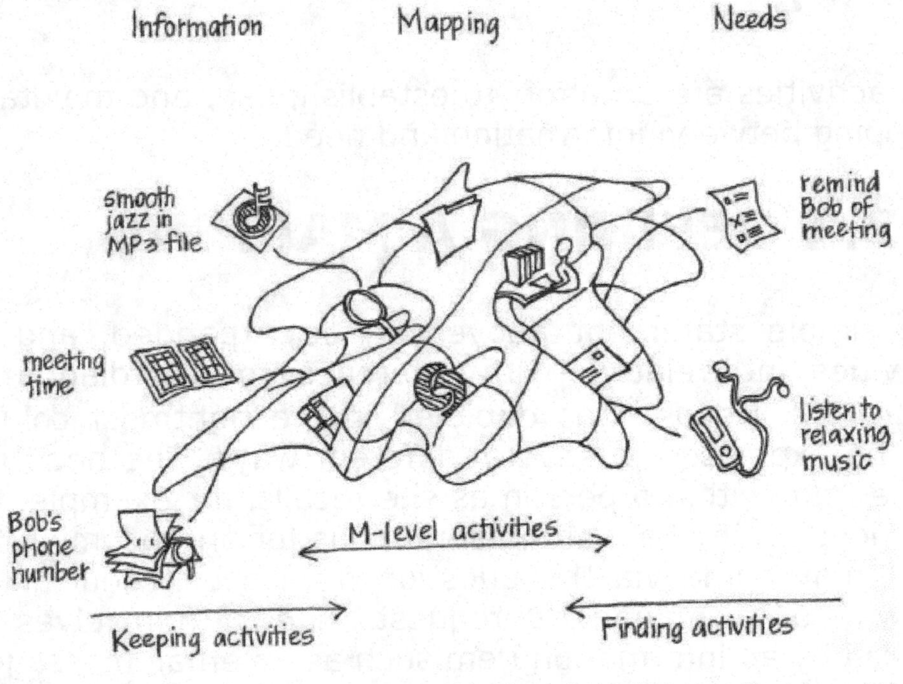

Figure 2.2: Information management activities viewed as an effort to establish, use and maintain a mapping between needs and information[90].

But parts of the mapping can be observed and manipulated. The folders of a filing system (whether for paper documents, electronic documents, email messages, or web references), the layout of a desktop (physical or virtual), and the choice of names, keywords, and other properties of information items all form parts of an observable fabric helping to knit need to information.

2.2.2 SIX ACTIVITIES OF PERSONAL INFORMATION MANAGEMENT

With respect to the mapping, we have two basic kinds of information management activity corresponding to the two directions in which the mapping can be traversed: Keeping activities attempt to take us from information encountered to anticipated need. Finding activities attempt to go in the other direction—from need to information.

Finding: From need to information. In their efforts to meet a need, people seek. People search, sort and browse. People scan through a results list or the listing of a folder's contents in an effort to recognize information items that relate to a need. These activities are all examples of finding activities. Finding is broadly defined to include both acts of new finding where there is no previous memory of having the needed information, and to include acts of re-finding. More broadly still, finding includes efforts to create the needed information as in "finding the right words" or "finding the right ideas."

Keeping: From information to need. Many events of daily life are roughly the converse of finding events. Instead of having a need for which we seek information, we have information in hand and must determine what, if anything, we need to do with this information. In organizations and as individuals we encounter and generate large amounts of information. Decisions and actions are much the same no matter the information or its source. Is the information at all relevant, or potentially useful? Do we have an anticipated need for this information? What are the costs of not having this information? Some information—tax-relevant information for past years, for example—must be kept even though the likelihood that a need for this information will arise is very small since the costs of not having this information, should the need arise, are very high[91].

A third set of PIM activities is focused on the mapping that connects need to information. These are collectively referred to as "meta-level activities."

Maintaining and organizing. How to … organize information for repeated use? … safeguard this information against loss? … insure that information is current and correct? … update formats to keep pace with changes in standards and in supporting tools? … insure that old information is deleted, archived or otherwise moved out the way? What about versions? What about duplicates and near-duplicates? These are all questions of maintenance and organization.

Managing privacy and the flow of information. We build roads of various kinds in order better for the right information to reach us at the right time. We subscribe to journals and periodicals. We pay for Internet connectivity. We cultivate friendships and collegial relationships. We also build walls to prevent the wrong people or their software proxies from compromising and corrupting our information. We select privacy settings on a service such as Facebook. We encrypt and password protect. We keep current on our services for protection against viruses. We are wary of unsolicited email. We also build walls in the form of folders and other groupings of information to avoid being overwhelmed by our information and to avoid being distracted by information that isn't currently relevant.

Measuring and evaluating. Choices are made in support of all the activities described so far. Schemes of organization are selected; strategies, policies and procedures are adopted; supporting tools are put in place. We then need to ask, periodically or continuously, "is it (the resulting mapping between information and need) working? Can it work even better? If so, what should change?" These questions depend both upon the measurements we're able to make and also on the evaluations we must make in cases where measurements (and the underlying objectives these measurements reflect) are in competition with one another.

Making sense of and using our information. Efforts to make sense are the most "meta" of meta-level activities. "What is this information telling me?" "Does it make sense?" The question can also be applied to choices made in each of the other meta-level activities. The question has broad application and reaches to deeper levels of understanding concerning ultimate goals and tradeoffs. We might hear ourselves saying something like "I understand what you want to do but it doesn't make sense." Choices that make sense with one need in mind may not make sense when other needs are also considered. Does the mapping make sense? Our information is now totally secure against unauthorized access but we can't easily access the information either. Does this make sense? We make sense of information. We use our senses. We also "make" and manipulate. Information is a thing to be piled and sorted, arranged and re-arranged. Information is a thing to be touched. Information is in the mapping. Information is also how we represent the needs of a mapping (including goals and constraints). Information, perhaps in the form of graphs, is how we represent a hierarchy of need. Information is how we represent the synergies and conflicts between needs. Information is how we represent the mapping itself. It's all information.

2.2.3 PUTTING MORE "META" INTO A BALANCED PRACTICE OF PIM

Finding and keeping activities need to complement each other. It makes little sense to take the trouble to keep information if this information can't be found again later when it's needed. Searching can dramatically improve the ease with which we find information but, without some effort to keep information—at least to note its existence and relevance to projects in our lives—we may forget even to look for this information later.

The effectiveness of keeping and finding activities depends, indirectly, on the effectiveness of an underlying organizational scheme and the strategies we apply to implement and maintain an organization over time. Lots of time can be wasted with bad schemes and bad strategies. Worse, information may be effectively lost even though it is right there—somewhere—neatly filed away. A bad organization can be worse than no organization at all.

Considerations of organizational schemes and strategies for keeping and organizing move us to the meta-level where the focus is more directly on the mapping between information and need. Which organizational schemes and strategies work best? How can we know? By what measurements and evaluations? Do our practices of maintenance ensure that the information, once found, is correct and current? Do we get the right version of a document? Or do we face a confusing "none of the above" choice between several documents versions? Can we manage the flow of information, incoming and outgoing, in ways that reduce the occasions to find and keep information? For example, subscriptions, RSS feeds, even our friends and colleagues can provide us with useful information we might otherwise need to find on our own (if we think to look in the first place).

But the meta-level activities are the "after" activities—the activities we postpone or never seem to have time for in a typically busy day. There are three general ways that better information management can leverage and be a part of our daily use of information.

Incidental. Given proper tool support many, if not most, measurements needed to evaluate our PIM practices can be collected automatically, as an incidental by-product of our daily use of information.

Incremental. A meta-level activity is easier to do if it can be done in small chunks spread over time. How can we accomplish something within a few seconds here and there when we're unwilling to take a longer period of time out of an already busy day? We do one kind of meta-level activity —managing the flow of information—every time we designate that an email message is "junk." An email application should use this designation to update and fine-tune its definition of what "junk" is to us. The designation of email messages as junk is an incremental activity. We can designate as many or as few as we want, depending on our time or inclination. With respect to management of information flow, we may ultimately want a more comprehensive privacy policy customized to our needs, with fine-grained distinctions drawn according to who wants what, when and why (under what circumstances). But if we had to create such a policy in a single sitting, we might never do so. And the policy created might not be that good either. Questions relating to privacy are more likely to get answered (with better answers) if these are distributed over time as the occasion arises. Similarly, maintenance actions —such as moving or deleting old information, updating or correcting information, removing duplicates and near-duplicates—these can also be distributed over time so that the incremental cost of completing a maintenance action is small.

Integrative. Meta-level activities are more likely to be done if these are integrated into other activities we do anyway and perhaps even like doing. A similar argument applies to exercise. We can exercise on a treadmill or by doing something we actually like doing, such as taking a nature walk or playing ultimate Frisbee. What about the organization of information? Why do so many of us talk about "getting organized" a lot more than we actually do it? Part of the answer is that organizing is a separate activity— made separate by the well-intentioned schemes of filing and tagging that are designed to support us. We do another activity all the time and we sometimes even enjoy it: we plan. Planning—whether planning a party, a vacation, or even a weekly meeting—can be fun and, anyway, it needs to be done. We will explore the possibility that, given the proper tool support, an effective organization of information can emerge as a natural by-product of the planning we must do in any case.

2.3 CONCLUSION

Information is sometimes packaged in information items that can be can be created, modified, stored, retrieved, given a name, tags, and other properties, moved, copied, distributed, deleted and otherwise manipulated. However, the ways of manipulating an information item vary according to an item's form, as supported by and sometimes defined by the tools we use such as applications to manage email, music, photographs or web browsing. Personal information is often scattered by its form into separate organizations for which we have developed distinct habits and strategies of PIM. Multiple forms of information exacerbate a situation of *information fragmentation* that is a central problem of PIM: the information we need is often widely scattered. A great deal of our time and effort is spent in managing information in different organizations on different devices and in gathering information together to get things done.

There are six senses in which information can be said to be personal and so an object of PIM. Information is personal to "me" if it is:

1. **Controlled by, owned by me.** Examples include email messages in our email accounts and files on our computer's hard drive devices.

2. **About me.** Examples include credit, medical, web browsing and library check-out histories.

3. **Directed toward me.** Examples include phone calls, drop-ins, TV ads, web ads and pop-ups.

4. **Sent (posted, provided) by me.** Examples include the email we send, post to a blog or a personal web site or publish in a report or an article.

5. **(Already) experienced by me.** Examples include web pages we have seen that remain on the Web or books we've read that remain in a library or TV and radio programs seen/heard that remain somewhere in "broadcast ether."

6. **Relevant (useful) to me.** This sixth sense of personal information includes information we are working with and also information "out there" that we would like to see. This sense of personal information also includes information that we do *not* want (ourselves or our family) to see, such as offensive material on the Web.

A personal space of information includes personal information in each of its senses. The PSI also includes various tools and other objects (virtual and visible) affecting the flow of information to, from, and through a PSI.

PIM activities are an effort to establish, use, and maintain a mapping between information and need. This basic statement leads to a framework in which we can place the following groupings of essential PIM activities.

Finding/re-finding activities move from need to information. This grouping includes explicit search queries as sent/posted to a web-based search service or to a computer desktop-based search facility. The grouping also includes various activities of sorting, browsing, and "nosing around" that people use to get back to information for re-access and reuse. And the grouping includes activities to publish (in a journal, for example), post (to a blog, wiki, or online forum, for example) or send (via email or surface mail, for example) information in an effort to meet one or more needs.

Keeping activities move from information to need. This grouping includes decisions concerning whether to make any effort to keep information for an anticipated use and, if so, decisions and actions concerning how to keep the information. Should information items be piled (where?), filed (which folder?), tagged (with which tags?), or committed to memory? Keeping also includes the decision to attend to information in the first place. Emails received invoke a sequence of keeping decisions: What is this? Do I need to deal with this now, or can a response wait until later? If later, should I flag, tag or file the message so that I can remember to deal with it later?

Meta-level activities focus on the mapping itself as a fabric weaving together information and need. Meta-level activities include efforts to organize (via schemes of piling, filing, or tagging), maintain (through backups, periodic cleanups, updates, and corrections), manage privacy and the flow of information (e.g.,through subscriptions, friendships, policies of disclosure),measure and evaluate (supporting tools and strategies, current and prospective, of a PIM practice) and make sense of personal information. Since meta-level activities are rarely forced on us by the events of a day, these activities invoke a more original sense of "meta" as in "after"—after keeping and finding activities, as an afterthought, or as activities placed in a receding "tomorrow" that never arrives. More "meta" can come into our daily practices of PIM through tools that are "incidental" in their automatic collection of PIM-relevant measures. We are also more likely to perform meta-level activities if these can be done in smaller increments (with lower costs of time and effort) or if these activities can be integrated into other activities we must do in any case such as planning.

---

[79]Buckland, M. (1991, p. 256).

[80]Sources used for definitions are the on-line services, Merriam-Webster OnLine (http://www.merriam-webster.com/dictionary/) and Wiktionary (http://en.wiktionary.org/wiki).

[81]Definitions come from Jones, W. (2007).

[82]UNC stands for Uniform Naming Convention and is a syntax and method for addressing files and folders in Microsoft Windows (http://en.wikipedia.org/wiki/Path_(computing)#Uniform_Naming_Convention). URI stands for Uniform Resource Identifier and is a generalization of the URL (Uniform Resource Locator). For the a hardcore definitive specification of URI syntax see http://tools.ietf.org/html/rfc3986. For a highly readable discussion of the URI, its purpose and related addressing initiatives such as XRI (Extensible Resource Identifier) and IRI (Internationalized Resource Identifier), see http://en.wikipedia.org/wiki/URI.

[83]Adopted from Jones, W. (2007).

[84]Note that even though information is, at least nominally, under the person's control, the rights of ownership for portions of this information are sometimes in dispute. In the context of a person's work inside a company or in collaboration with others, for example, it is often unclear who owns what information.

[85]PSI is frequently used as the Roman alphabet spelling of the Greek letter which, in turn, is frequently associated with psychology. The Merriam-Webster OnLine dictionary defines "psychology" as the "science of mind and behavior."

Psyche has its origins in the ancient Greek word for breath, essence of life or soul.

[86]Illustration by Elizabeth Boling.

[87]Karger and Quan (2004) defined a "collection" broadly to include a variety of objects, ranging from menus to portals to public taxonomies. Boardman and Sasse (2004), in contrast, defined a collection of personal information to be "a self-contained set of items. Typically, the members of a collection share a particular technological format and are accessed through a particular application."

[88]In a personal communication, one researcher told me she uses 12 separate custom properties and "lives by" her EndNote database.

[89]For a more complete discussion of need in an informational context, see Naumer and Fisher (2010).

[90]Figure 2.2 is an illustration done by Elizabeth Boling and is a variation of a figure that first appeared in Jones, W. (2007).

[91]For a discussion of the calculus of keeping and the consideration of costs of a false positive (keeping information that proves useless) vs. a miss (not keeping information what is later needed), see (Jones, W., 2004).

CHAPTER 3
Our Information, Always at Hand

The names we use for our computing devices are descriptive for their situations of use. In the beginning of personal computing, there were desktop computers. Desktop computers, if not always literally atop a desktop, are closely tied to a physical desktop or some item of furniture providing a sturdy, flat surface.

Later came the laptop—a computer that could be placed atop our laps and used in many other places besides the desktop of an office or a home.

Early laptops were a complement to, not a replacement of, the desktop computer. Compared with desktop computers, early laptop computers were considerably slower, had less memory, less disk space, smaller screens and tiny ("chicklet") keyboards. But laptops got better.

For many of us, the laptop is now the primary computer. The laptop on its own may not be ideal but it is "good enough." We occasionally dock to desktop display and a full-size keyboard. The rest of the time, we're mobile. We take our laptops from the office to home and to coffee shops and meeting rooms in between. We take our laptops as we travel.

But even if the laptop unchains us from our own desktops, we remain encumbered. The laptop and also a carrying backpack or briefcase have become our constant companions. At airports we take our laptops out to join a procession of other laptops, one laptop per plastic tub, wending their way through the x-ray machine. And laptop use requires a stable platform of some kind—if not our literal laps then a tabletop or somebody's desk.

Now we have computing devices referred to variously as "smartphones," "Handheld PCs," Personal digital assistants (PDAs)[92], or, simply, "palmtops." The term *palmtop* is apt. We place these devices in the palm of our hand. We're no longer tied to a desktop. Nor are we tied to our laps or the need to sit down[93].

We can carry a palmtop with us no matter where we go, even on occasions when a laptop might stay home. Moreover, the palmtop has *social affordances*[94] that are missing from the laptop. Whether good or bad, people use their palmtops in situations where use of a laptop might be awkward or appear downright strange. Consider the following situations:

1. standing on the side-lines at a child's soccer game;

2. standing in an elevator; and

3. standing (or sitting) at a cocktail party.

Use a laptop? Not likely. Use a palmtop device such as an iPhone, an Android, a Windows Mobile phone or a Blackberry? Whether we would do so, we've doubtless seen others do so and without attracting attention.

Palmtops are take-everywhere, use-anywhere for nearly everything—computer, camera, phone, song player, remote control and much more, all rolled into one. In support of this device convergence is the notion of "good enough." People are often willing to trade some of the features of a higher-end device for the convenience of a single, smaller device that delivers not one but many functions. Even serious photographers, for example, sometimes trade away some quality for the convenience of a camera built-in to a cell phone they will carry anyway[95].

Palmtops of increasing power—connected to the Internet and enhanced by the optional, occasional use of larger screen, keyboard and other peripherals—might eventually displace the laptop as a primary computing platform in a manner similar to the laptop's displacement of the desktop computer. Radical convergence? All our computing needs in purse or pocket? Some people are almost there.

Consider Larry. He moves from meeting to meeting throughout his day and prefers to travel light with only his palmtop, which he easily stows in pant or vest pocket. He uses his palmtop primarily for quick look up ("Where is my next meeting?"), short communications (via email, texting and occasionally voice) and simple note-taking (which he has become quite adept at doing on his palmtop). He still has a laptop but mostly this now stays parked—at home in the evenings and in his (usually vacant) office during the day. For most of his day, Larry needs only one device.

However, other developments in what might be called "form factor specialization" work against such a radical convergence of information needs to a single palmtop device. For example, the Kindle and the iPad occupy points in-between the laptop and the palmtop both in size and in situations of use. Use them at a party? Probably not. Even carrying them to the party might be awkward. Use them while standing at a child's soccer game or waiting for a bus? Quite possibly.

Consider Joan. She has been issued a desktop computer and a laptop through her job and has another laptop of her own for non-work use. She also has an iPhone, iPad and a Kindle. She makes special use of each. She likes the Kindle, for example, because it is just small enough to fit into her coat pocket, is easy to read from and has a multi-day battery life. Joan also has several digital cameras which she uses in her role as the photographer for her son's soccer team. There is no device convergence for Joan.

Larry and Joan use decidedly different constellations of devices. Even so, they share in common a nearly constant 24x7 access to digital information. This chapter is not primarily about gadgetry or enabling technologies. This chapter is about the challenges and the opportunities of PIM in a world where our information—in all of the six senses discussed in Chapter 2—is, quite literally, always at hand.

The theme, "Our information, always at hand," connects to two trends that carry us into the future by simple extrapolation.

1. *Physical meets digital (and everything is logged).* Once there was little to connect our digital, on-line reality with our physical reality. Now the gap is bridged. The palmtop connects to digital storage and to the Internet on one side. The palmtop provides the means to measure and control our physical reality on the other side. Our every action can be logged. How is this log used later? And by whom?

2. *Always connected (and always on call).* We are always, everywhere subject to interruption through various modes of communication ranging from phone calls to text messages to email alerts. When others are not interrupting us, we may interrupt ourselves—for example, to add a reminder to our calendar or to check a sports score. To the good, we are no longer anchored to a desk. We can do nearly anything information-related, no matter when or where we are. To the bad, we may be operating in a state of constant overstimulation and distraction. Are we constantly busy but never seem to get anything done?

As we consider each theme, discussion will speak of a palmtop device as the means for sending and receiving, recording and retrieving information. If you are more like Joan than Larry in the scenarios above, please make the appropriate substitutions according to your own constellation of devices.

3.1 PHYSICAL MEETS DIGITAL

The palmtop is a constant companion. It's the thing together with keys and wallet that we carry with us whenever we leave home. It's the thing that may soon replace keys and wallet. The palmtop goes with us not only outside the home but inside as well. We are not dressed without it. It lies within reach even when we are undressed. It is on the night stand as we sleep.

An ordinary cell phone—i.e., one that does little else but place and receive telephone calls—already has a similar place of honor in the lives of many people. The palmtop as constant companion does much more.

Time-based reminders are nothing new. But now reminders can trigger for location as well as in "don't forget to pick up the prescription" (while you are already near the pharmacy). A great many information needs are location-specific ("is there a hardware store nearby?") and searches augmented by the context of both time and location (current or projected) promise to return much better results[96].

A palmtop connected supports a growing diversity of communication modes: tweeting; Email messaging; text messaging; Blog posting; Web-page browsing. Built-in cameras make it easy for people to send not only pictures of their surroundings but also self-portraits and emotional expressions[97]. People send pictures for fun ("here are pictures of our hike yesterday") and for function (a picture of a milk container sent to a spouse could serve as a reminder to get groceries on the way home from work). People might tell a story "live" as it unfolds through a multimedia presentation that includes text, photos, sound and video[98].

The melding of physical and digital realities creates new opportunities for socialization[99]. We may opt in to services[100] so that others can learn of our current physical location. We may soon "face" a situation where others can identify us in public even without our opt-in. A photo taken, for example, may provide the basis for a match to an on-line profile of ourselves as maintained, for example, in Facebook. Through such identification, the stranger across the room in a bar or coffee shop may then be able to find out a great deal about us without our knowledge or any opt-in.

The palmtop connects us not only to other people but also to physical objects. Using variations in radio-frequency identification (RFID), for example, a palmtop might track the location of our jewelry, keys or a TV remote[101].

Even better, the palmtop can replace our remotes. The palmtop as a "universal remote" gives us a reach far beyond the limits of our physical selves. Consider the hundreds of applications one can already download for control of televisions, garage doors, sound systems, video games, lighting, sprinkler systems, presentation projectors and much more[102]. The palmtop can set or disable our security system at home. The palmtop can be the key that unlocks the door to our house or automobile. Using standards such as Bluetooth and Near Field Communication (NFC)[103] our palmtop devices might handshake with a variety of devices in our physical space. Our palmtop can readily become a remote for some devices and, in the case of other non-electronic devices, a provider of Web-based information for manual control of the device.

3.1.1 ACCESSORIZE! THE WATCH WATCH AND OTHER WEARABLE

DEVICES OF INPUT AND OUTPUT

We can also assume that technologies will bridge two additional physical/digital gaps—those for the input to and output from the palmtop itself.

The palmtop will take our voice commands for immediate action ("text a reminder to Mark about the meeting today at 3 pm") and longer, less constrained voice notes for "near-time" transcription[104]. The palmtop may soon support the use of a projected or even "air" keyboard[105]. And the palmtop may support the use of a projected display for shared output and for shared input[106]. People gathered around the display might, for example, collaboratively explore a map or author a presentation slide or the plans for an office layout.

Similar to the laptop, the palmtop will dock for use with conventional I/O devices—keyboards, display screens, printers, etc. (The palmtop will also dock at nighttime for re-charging and also, optionally, for the backup of its contents either to a local device or to the Web or both[107].)

But does the palmtop accessorize? Does it work with other items we wear or routinely carry? Think, for example, of a "watch" watch[108], not as a bulky device that works on its own but as a sleek fashionable device with a Bluetooth connection to the palmtop. The watch-watch lets us watch much more than just the time of day. The watch-watch tells us the weather outside, the price of stocks on our "watch list," news alerts, traffic status, etc. The watch-watch reminds and notifies.

The watch-watch is input to as well as output from the palmtop so that the palmtop, for much of our day, can stay stowed in pocket or purse as we move about. On the input side, the watch-watch measures body temperature, heart rate, blood pressure and overall levels of physical activity.

The watch-watch might even measure air quality and raise alerts when levels of CO or ozone are too high[109].

The watch-watch also takes as input our voice commands and notes. The watch-watch is the proverbial "two-way wrist radio" of the Dick Tracy comic strip[110]. The watch-watch acts on our command to "call Julie" and then serves as both microphone and speaker for the conversation that follows.

Moving beyond the watch, we can think of other fashion accessories that might be modified to do double duty as an interface to the palmtop. The medallion on a necklace or chain, for example, or the buckle on a belt or the rims on glasses[111] might take snapshots as we move through our day—in much the same manner as the bulkier SenseCam is able to do today[112]. Snapshots sent to the palmtop and then possibly onto the Web might then be analyzed to provide, for example, information concerning the name, background and our connection to the person we are currently talking to at a cocktail party where information is sent back discreetly to an ear bud for our private listening. Farther out, a necklace or necktie may capture and support recognition of sub-vocal speech so that we can mouth commands or notes to our palmtops even in public spaces such as a favorite coffee shop[113].

3.1.2 THE CHALLENGES OF PRIVACY AND SECURITY

There are obvious dangers in a world where the local physical so readily integrates with the global digital and so many of our daily activities can be recorded for possible Web-wide access. In general, people are unaware of the extent to which personal information sent via current public "Wi-Fi" networks (802.11-based wireless networks) is potentially available to others within broadcast range[114].

Even information that is only seen by its intended recipient can reveal more than we realize or care to disclose —especially when sent "on the go" and on the spur of the moment. This is true, in particular, for pictures. We may not want to disclose the location at which a photograph was taken. We may be especially protective concerning information about our children. Some Web services (e.g., Flickr) now make it easier for people to filter out location information from pictures that are posted[115].

We must also recognize the possibility that in any public setting we can appear in the photo taken by a security camera or we may happen into the background of a photo taken by someone else. Preservation of privacy and anonymity in public places was never assured and certainly isn't now[116]. Cameras outside on gates, inside in convenience stores, cameras in the hands of many people at a sporting event—we can never be sure we aren't being recorded. As techniques of digital editing continue to improve there is even a risk that someone can be "inserted" into the photos for places where they were not.

Legal protections in a digital world are imperfect and in flux. Can email information be subpoenaed? Probably. What about data that records our physical location? Possibly not[117]. Rules and regulations are a work in progress. All the while, as recording devices proliferate and storage costs plummet, the amount of data about us and our communications that *might* be used against us (fairly or unfairly) continues to grow[118]. In such a world, there may be value in being able to provide our own record—our own alibi so to speak[119].

3.1.3 LIFELOGGING

The palmtop and accessories as constant companions raises the possibility that we might record our lives even as we are living them. The result has been called a *lifelog*. Recent related efforts include the now-cancelled Darpa "Lifelog" project[120], MyLifeBlts[121], CARPE[122], and efforts by Steve Mann to design EyeTap and other wearable devices of capture and computing[123]. "Memories for Life" has become a U.K. Grand Challenge in Computing[124]. Visions of total recall[125] are inspired by advances in technology and by notions that computers with their high-volume capacities of rapid encoding, durable storage and later literal retrieval might play a complementary role in relation to human memory[126].

Technologies of capture and storage make the realization of a lifelog, in some form, technically feasible. By some projections, support for 24x7 full-motion video may not be far away[127].

We are then left to consider not merely "how" questions of basic technical feasibility but additional "why," "how" and "what" questions. Why record? For what purposes? How is information in a life log accessed and used? And, what is actually recorded?

Why Record?

In assessing the potential benefits of lifelogging, Sellen and Whittaker (2010) referred to the "the 5 Rs"[128]:

1. **Recollecting** (e.g., names of people we encountered or likely last location of something misplaced).

2. **Reminiscing** (as a special case of recollecting, the re-experiencing of past events such as vacations or fun outings).

3. **Retrieving** (a specific information item such as a document or a photograph).

4. **Reflecting** (e.g., on our behavior in past situations or our use of time—often with an intention to do better in the future).

5. **Remembering intentions** (e.g., our commitments to meet someone or our promise to complete a task by a certain time).

The preservation of digital photographs or video recordings over time for later viewing carries its own set of issues[129]. But Sellen and Whittaker went a step further to note that, even given this preservation, the connection of an image or recording to the person—its evocative potential, we might say—depends upon the person's memory and this too is subject to decay with the passage of time. A picture of a sunset that meant so much to us at the time we took the photo may be "just another sunset" when viewed again ten years later.

Indeed, Sellen et al. (2007) in a study of SenseCam images, observed a decline over time in the power of images to spark remembering. However, they note that even after an image loses its ability to evoke a memory in the person involved, the image can still help the person to "know" that something must have happened (i.e., "I must have been at John's birthday party since there I am in the picture"). Conversely, we must note the potential for falsified photographs or videos to "recover" a memory of an event that never occurred[130].

Perhaps more likely is that people simply don't consult their lifelog—even in situations where it might be helpful. With respect to retrieving, people may simply forget to look in the first place[131]. Or people may settle for imperfect, approximate knowledge if quickly retrieved from their own internal memories in preference to more accurate, complete knowledge that might be gleaned from an external source but only with additional time and effort[132]. People may decide that what they can remember is "good enough" and that retrieval from a lifelog is not worth effort.

How is the log accessed?

We note that even as a lifelog potentially provides the 5 Rs of benefit listed above, it may pose its own retrieval challenges. How shall we access our lifelogs? Consider, for example, a streaming, full-motion video as lifelog. Obviously, we can't view from start to finish. We need points of access into the log.

Time is one basis for organizing and accessing a lifelog. Both the MEMOIRS system[133] and LifeStreams[134] use time as a primary means of organization. Documents and other information items (appointments, for example) are "events" to be placed in sequence according to time of occurrence. LifeStreams went a step further by placing intentions (appointments, deadlines) as future events in the time ordered stream.

But time is an abstract concept and our memories for when a sought-for event actually occurred can themselves quickly decay with the passage of time[135]. We recall that our meeting with a friend happened "yesterday" or "in the middle of last week" or "sometime in early June" or "sometime in the fall of 2009." Unless we can anchor the memory for an event to another event with an established date such as "9/11," our memories for the time of the event are apt to get increasingly fuzzy the farther back in time this event occurred.

Our palmtops will be able to mark not only by time but also by physical location. Location may sometimes be a more effective basis for retrieval. We can think of events in our lives where our memory for location is exact ("that happened at the apartment I had in Somerville") but our memories for the time are at best approximate ("It must have happened sometime during the two years that I lived there"). Unfortunately, many events for which we might want to consult a lifelog are likely to happen in the same places—an office, for example, or a favorite coffee shop—so that location alone has low precision as a retrieval cue.

A general ideal of re-finding support, whether the targeted item is a document or an event in a lifelog, is that anything we recall and express concerning the item brings us a little closer to its retrieval. This ideal argues for a lifelog in which events are richly inter-connected and indexed with the words, pictures and attributes we would likely associate with these events.

What is recorded?

A full-motion video may seem like the gold standard for lifelogging but what does this record concerning our actual interactions? How well does such a video record the emails, text messages and tweets that we send? How well does it record the Web pages we visit, the on-line orders we place or the changes we make to a document? More important, is it realistic for us to create a complete video recording of our lives even if technically feasible? Would we want to?

In an earlier age when the technical challenges of capture and the costs of digital storage were far greater, both Memoirs and Lifestreams settled upon the generalized notion of the document as the thing to record. In Lifestreams, for example, an email sent, phone call made, a Web page bookmarked—each of these results in a document, which is placed in the time-ordered lifestream according to the date/time of its creation. As the user edited a conventional document, this resulted in a new version which was also placed in the lifestream.

But what if we want a document to have two times? The first time might be when the document was initially created; the second might be the time it was last modified or possibly even a future time of anticipated use (e.g., "at the status meeting next Tuesday"). To accomplish this, in MEMOIRS or LifeStreams, we must make a second (and third and fourth ...) copy. The approach is problematic and even more so in situations where an item is accessed by several different people and repeatedly. Whose stream does the document go into?

Moreover, the concept of document is problematic. We live in an age of Web-based information where information is increasingly hyperlinked and the where the thing we see and work with may be generated dynamically. We struggle to define the document[136].

The alternative, as discussed in Chapter 2, is to think in terms of entry points into a vast "soup" of information. An entry point has its URI. We may think in terms of "opening" a document or some other item of information. For example, we may wish to open marketing report that we worked with yesterday. But our request to open this document translates into a tool-specific request to "return something" in association with the specified URI. What we actually experience and the extent to which what we experience is the "same" document we worked with yesterday will depend upon a variety of factors including the tool we use, its supporting device (laptop? palmtop?) and the actions taken by other people in association with this URI since yesterday.

It then doesn't make sense to record a "document" per se in the log. An alternative is to record the event of our having taken some action (e.g., "open," "close," "create," "delete," "modify") in association with some item as specified by its URI. An event in the log is then simply a statement. We might think in terms of the subject-predicate-object statements which are the atoms of the resource definition framework (RDF)[137].

- **Subject**. In our logs, we are always the subject of the events that transpire. In situations of collaborative work, the subject will vary to represent, for example, the succession of team members who modify a document. A person, as the subject of an event, can also be addressed by a URI[138].

- **Verb (predicate)**. We create and destroy (delete) documents. We send and receive email messages. We make and cancel appointments. We open and close windows containing a range of items from documents to email messages to Web pages[139].

- **Object**. An object is referenced through its address, i.e., its URI.

Additional attributes to record per event include:

- time of occurrence;

- location of occurrence; and

- tool and device involved in the recording of an event.

Other attributes might also be recorded per event to represent aspects of the digital "location" (vs. physical location) in which an event occurs. What other items have recently been opened? Are these still in view (and shaping our experience of the item referenced in the current event)? But in a proper logging of events, this contextual information might also be derived from previous events in the log.

When considering a schema to define the log and its events, other considerations also apply. For example, it is likely that the log will need to be maintained by several different tools both in accordance with our changing preferences and also in accordance with the device we are currently using. The schema needs to allow, therefore, for the persistence of tool-specific attributes in association with each event[140].

Other variations to consider are as follows.

An event might be recorded in two separate logs—one in association with its subject URI and the other in association with its object URI. We then have a kind of "double bookkeeping." The sequence of events for a subject tells us a story of what the "URI" (typically referencing a person) has done. The sequence of events for an object tells us a story of what's been done to the object (e.g., to the referenced document or Web page). Such a log acts as a revision history for its object.

Events might even become items in their own right with associated URIs. This would allow us to comment on an event after the fact and to add, retrospectively, additional attributes for the event. Comments and other attributes are part of a new event, placed in association with a past event without violating the integrity of its original recording.

Sample log events (with URIs augmented by more meaningful display names) are depicted in Table 3.1. The log needs a name to be distinguished from other variations of logging (such as the "document in the log" approach taken by LifeStream and Memoirs). We'll call it the *item experience log*, or *i.e.log* for short[141].

Table 3.1: A depiction for a portion of an i.e.log.

Action	Address	Type	Display Name	Tool- or event-type-specific Attributes
Create	<URI>	Appointment	"Daughter's soccer game"	Start-time, End-time
...				
Create	<URI>	Photograph	< optional>	
Send	<URI>	Email message	"She just scored!"	Recipients

3.1.4 THE USES OF AN I.E.LOG

The idea behind the i.e.log is simple:

- Decide upon a set of noteworthy actions to represent our interactions with information or, more generally, within any "thing" that can be addressed by a URI. Noteworthy actions include Create, Destroy (Delete), Send, Receive, Open, Close, Modify, Move, etc.

- Each time one of these actions is done, record an event in the log as a statement with us as subject (as represented by a URI), the action as a predicate (verb) and the object involved (document, email message, Web page) represented by its URI.

- Record additional attributes per event to describe time, physical location and tool/device involved. Optionally, also record friendly display names for the object and action of an event.

The i.e.log is a cross-device, platform-independent representation of our activities across various tools, applications and devices. The i.e.log has many uses:

- **A general auto-complete**. Type in a few characters, see suggested completions and select one. This basic "auto-complete" facility is already present in some contexts but not others. Auto-complete helps us in the completion of a Web address, an email address or a search query. A more general auto-complete[142] might provide fast access to Web pages, files, email messages, email addresses for people and anything else addressable by a URI.

- **Indexing and full-text search for refinding**. A more complete, content-based or "full-text" search requires the support of an index for speed. In turn, an index for personal search needs to have scope. We are not interested in a search of "all" files, email messages or Web pages. Rather, we want to return a file, email message or Web page we've viewed (visited) before. The i.e.log provides a good way to establish this scope.

- **Back-ups and updates**. An i.e.log provides scope not only for indexing but also back-ups and updates. Imagine a backup of our information that is inclusive of *all* our personal information. Backups would cover not only the information on a given device or a specific file system but, more generally, also the information we create through a service like Gmail, Facebook or Evernote. Likewise, the i.e.log establishes a manageable scope for the updates—especially of status information about ourselves (changes in address, job and marital status).

- **Associative, synergistic retrieval**. People return to information—they *refind*—in distinctly different ways depending upon various factors including the item involved and the person's familiarity with this item and its location. People browse or navigate to some items; they search to others. Together, the sequence of items referenced in the i.e.log can support both modes. In Table 3.1, for example, the photograph taken of a daughter scoring a goal at a soccer game provides an excellent landmark for navigation to nearby events such as the email sent to our spouse. Conversely, the text of the email message provides searchable content for the location of the photograph which otherwise might not "speak for itself " through comments we don't take the time to make.

- **A basis for retrospective journaling and sharing**. As we review events in our i.e.log we may be prompted to comment (a new event). We may wish to post selected events or the items involved (e.g., photographs taken) for sharing on a social Web site such as Facebook. Here too, we're likely to make comments. Many of us may have resolved, more than once, to keep a diary or a journal of life's events and then, with neither time nor energy left at the end of a busy day, failed to do so. But a log of events automatically recorded and interconnected through our sharing and commentary may give us a journal as an incidental by-product of the activities we must do in any case.

- **Self-trackers and the quantified self** [143]. "Know thyself " is inscribed in the Temple of Apollo at Delphi. "The unexamlned life is not worth living," Socrates is reported to have said[144]. A personal desire to reflect upon and learn from our life's events is not new. But with our information and the means to track informational interactions always at hand, we have the potential for a much more rigorous, quantified tracking and correlation among the life events. An i.e.log might potentially help us to objectively answer questions such as "Do I generally get more or less work done after visiting Starbucks?" or "When is the best time of day to make investment decisions?" or "Where did the time go today?" An i.e.log (especially as fed by a "watch-watch") might track our levels of physical activity through the day as a way of telling us how much exercise we're getting and as a way to motivate us to exercise more[145].

3.2 CONSTANTLY CONNECTED (AND CONSTANTLY ON CALL)

Our information always at hand means that many conventional barriers, many "walls," between different regions of our lives are removed. Work at home. Arrange a social event at work. Check email while on vacation or at a dinner. Read or work on a marketing report while watching TV. Many activities, many sides to our lives, all mixed together.

New modes of communication also mean new informational roads: In-person, phone, email, texting, tweets and Facebook posts. Traffic down these roads moves in both directions. Always connected means, in one way or another, always on call. We can be interrupted. Other people interrupt us through any of several modes of communication. Our devices and tools interrupt us. We interrupt ourselves ... even in the middle of another interruption[146].

Interruptions bring a new dimension to the pervasive PIM problem of fragmentation as discussed in Chapters 1 and 2. Our information is scattered into bits and pieces by the many tools we use. Our time too, and our thinking, are fragmented into many small slices scattered between separate requests, tasks and to-dos.

This section is first about caveats: we consider the limits, downsides and outright dangers of multi-tasking. This section is last about possibilities. Our information always at hand opens up new opportunities to stay informed, work smarter and get more things done with our precious time.

3.2.1 MULTI-TASKING "BUSYNESS"[147]

"One thing at a time." The phrase is invoked most often when our efforts to do more than one thing are manifestly not working. The phrase is often disregarded in the very next breath. Why not do more than one thing at a time if we can? Time is short; our to-do lists are long. Why not "multi-task"[148]?

But what is multi-tasking? Can we really do more than one thing at a time? Answers depend upon the tasks—the things being done—and also on the period of time. Two things in the same second? Of course. At least, some things. We breathe; our hearts beat; we walk; we think—all in the same instance.

Over a longer period of time—a half hour, for example—it is clear that we multi-task by any reasonable definition of the tasks or things being done. The ring of the phone, the knock at the door, the tone indicating a new message—each event acts to draw our attention away from one task and onto another. In many situations, people face a constant stream of interruptions. Over the period of a half hour or so, attention may shift among several tasks[149].

By giving freedom of definition first to the time interval and second to the thing being done, we uncover two cases of what are commonly referred to as "multi-tasking"[150].

1. **Task-switching.** In many instances of apparent multi-tasking we are, instead, switching from one task to another. Doing homework or responding to email while watching a show on TV? We are not doing both tasks at the same time. Instead, we are switching our attention between the two. For most of us, interruptions are part of our jobs and our lives so that we task-switch of necessity. Task-switching may be a reality but it is not an ideal. Task-switching can be very costly as measured by cognitive effort, speed and the quality or accuracy of task outcome[151]. Switching involves additional overhead to monitor each task and its current state of completion. Switching is effortful. It takes time to resume the primary task after a switch. Two tasks interleaved are apt to be done more poorly and to take longer to complete than if each were done in succession. As we attempt to process email while watching TV, we may end up sending poorly worded email messages and later be unable to recall what we were watching on TV.

2. **Automaticity**[152]. In cases of automaticity, one task is the focus of attention; one or more additional "tasks" are done automatically. Consider walking or driving a

familiar route. The task is nearly automatic in its performance. We can use the time also to think about an upcoming meeting at work or to listen to a news show on the radio. Certainly one secondary task we perform nearly constantly, regardless of our primary task, is monitoring. We monitor for sudden movements on the periphery, the cry of our children or the mention of our name. We do so automatically, without conscious effort, without volition. When one task is performed automatically or nearly so, it may seem that we can focus on another task simultaneously with little decrement to the performance of either task[153]. But notice how quickly the calculus of attention can shift. In an argument with a companion or if we're thinking about a complicated problem, we may slow the pace of our walking or driving. Worse, we may be less likely to notice an oncoming danger. We may not even hear someone call our name. Conversely, as our walking turns strenuous on an uphill or as we drive in a downpour, we're likely to suspend our conversation or our thinking about the upcoming meeting.

Some people might think that the use of a hands-free headset to talk with someone over the phone while driving is comparable to talking with the person sitting in a passenger seat. Of course we talk to the person sitting next to us; why not this same person connected via palmtop as long as our hands and eyes are still free for driving? There is, however, one critical difference between these two situations: The passenger next to us shares our driving context. A good passenger will stop talking when the driving gets tricky and may even help us out ("watch out for that car merging into our lane"); the same person talking with us over the phone doesn't share our context and may not even know we're driving.

Is a younger generation raised in an age of digital information innately better able to multi-task? Can the rest of us acquire a general skill of multi-tasking with practice? Apparent evidence in favor of either possibility invariably points to one of the two situations above. Either people are switching rapidly between tasks or they have completed one task sufficiently often as to do so now automatically or nearly so[154 155 156].

Why not develop automaticity for an activity like "reading and responding to email?" In truth, completion of any real-world task involves a mix of different actions and skills. Our actions to open an email or to read a routine status report may be highly practiced and nearly automatic. But the thinking involved in responding to a new request is not automated and, by its nature (it is new) can't be[157]. We must then consider the possibility that in cases of apparent multi-tasking—texting while conversing with friends over dinner, for example—we may be in "automatic" mode with respect to one or both activities. Exchanges proceed in parallel without apparent disruption to either only as long performance on these tasks is routine and superficial. In other words, we (no matter our age), multi-task only by "dumbing down."

What about texting or the manual entry of a phone number while driving a familiar route? If the driving task is automated, can't we do the other task? No. First, our driving can never be fully automated. No matter how routine the route or perfect the conditions, we must always be prepared to handle non-routine or, even, emergency situations. Our car gets a flat tire. Or a child, not looking, crosses the path of the car. In these cases, our attention must shift immediately from automatic to focused and conscious. More important, no matter the automaticity of the one task, problems arise if both tasks compete for the same physical resources. Eyes that should be on the road and hands that should be on the steering wheel, are engaged elsewhere—in a very dangerous form of task switching.

3.2.2 REALLY GETTING REAL THINGS DONE

We are still left with many situations in life where there is little apparent alternative but to attempt to multitask. "One thing at a time?" How is this possible in a world where there are far too many things that need to get done and far too little time in which to do them? Here are some practical guidelines to consider in your own practice of PIM.

- **Reduce the occurrence of task-switching.** Avoid situations of "busyness" in which you are switching constantly from one task (e.g., watching a TV program) to another (responding to email). Block out times for task completion. Set expectations. Close the door. Turn off email. Manage your manager. Be proactive, not reactive. These and other like-minded imprecations each serve to reduce the occurrence of task-switching.

- **Reduce the cost of task-switching.** At the same time, some task switching can't be avoided. The knock at the door may be someone important. We interrupt ourselves with a thought or a to-do that, even if unrelated to the task at hand, needs to be noted before it's forgotten. There are two general ways to minimize the costs of task-switching.

  1. **Minimize the time spent on the interrupting task**. Keep a paper notebook close at hand, send yourself email, write things in an electronic document or spreadsheet, use a special "note-this" utility. Each offers a relatively fast way to "capture" a thought or to-do and then to return quickly to the task at hand.

2. **Minimize the time needed to resume the primary task.** Resumption of a task after an interruption can take many minutes as we reassemble the materials of the task (e.g., the papers of a physical desktop or the windows of a computer desktop) and our memories for the state of the task when interrupted. Or resumption may not happen until much later[158]. Better is to structure a task so that its state at interruption is more stable or more readily preserved. Simon, H. (1969) used the example of a watchmaker to illustrate the importance of stable subassemblies. The famous, 19th century explorer, Sir Richard Francis Burton, was known to keep a separate desk in his home study for each of the projects he was actively working on[159].

- **Switch tasks to get "unstuck."** On the other hand, if we are "spinning our wheels" on a task and making little progress, then interrupting ourselves may be just the right thing to do. Especially a physical activity such as going for a walk or taking a swim may actually accomplish two purposes in one effort: the exercise is good and we're jolted out of a state that is not productive.

Looking for win/win through mutualism. Observe yourself and your performance as you complete tasks. Look for real synergies among the things to be done. Consider a biological metaphor. Tasks frequently compete with one another for your time, energy and attention. But in cases of "task commensalism," the performance of one task does little to impact the performance of another. In the previous section, we considered cases where the work of one task was sufficiently automated so as to be, so to speak, in the hands and feet, thus freeing our mind to engage in thinking related to another task. We walk or drive a familiar route while thinking of an upcoming meeting for example.

Even better are situations of "task mutualism" where two tasks are performed with mutual benefit to each or, alternatively, where one activity serves two or more ends. There is often a strong social element in such activities. We post a photo to Facebook or Flickr together with an explanatory caption to share with our friends and family. But pictures are there later for us to look at as well (as long as Facebook and Flickr don't go away). And the captions may prove invaluable to us as our memories for the circumstances around taking the picture have faded.

Consider the several ends served by the simple act of emailing a Web link to an interested colleague. A relationship is strengthened. He or she may return the favor. Moreover, a useful exchange may ensue. Similarly, some people blog as a way of "thinking out loud" as they grapple with a complicated issue about which they must write an article or a term paper. In the course of exchanging email messages or posting to a blog, a person may discover that the material generated puts them well on their way to the completion of the article or term paper.

Or consider the classic case of golfing with a friend or business associate. The experience of golfing is likely more pleasurable for the companionship. Moreover, issues may be discussed and resolved during the golf game that would not be so easily discussed in a more formal meeting explicitly scheduled for this purpose. Some tasks, such as dining, combine well with a number of other tasks, while other tasks such as reading or playing video games, do not combine well with other activities[160].

3.3 CONCLUSION

This chapter has looked at the challenges and the opportunities of a world in which our information is, "always at hand." Sophisticated computing devices we carry and wear mean our physical and digital worlds combine and sometimes collide. We need to take steps to insure that information personal to us is secure against unauthorized access or outright theft. However, given the ubiquity of cameras and other recording devices there may be little we can do to maintain our personal privacy in public settings. Instead, we can at least maintain our own record "for the record."

An i.e. (item event) log as a recording of basic actions we take towards our information (e.g., open, close, create, delete) can potentially be cheaply captured and recorded. The i.e.log provides a basis for auto-complete, more comprehensive full-text searching, back-ups, and updates. Each activity can be scoped to include all and only those information items that have become personal to us through our logged interactions with them. Events in a sequence can provide complementary support to each other with respect to the refinding methods of navigation (browsing) and search.

Information and communication are two sides of the same coin. Information always at hand means we are constantly connected. And connections are a two-way road. We can be interrupted in our primary task by people on the other side of the world with little awareness of our current context. We interrupt ourselves.

Old barriers, old walls fall. We can work anywhere; we can play anywhere. When there are many things to be done and little time to do them we try to multi-task. However, in cases of apparent multi-tasking one of the following is likely to be true.

1. We are switching, perhaps rapidly, between tasks.

2. One task is so well-practiced and routine so as to be done automatically or nearly so.

Task switching is costly—as measured by extra effort, total task completion time and the reduced quality of completed tasks. When we send email while watching TV we may send poorly worded email messages and still not enjoy or later remember the TV program we're watching.

Automaticity is highly specific. There is no such thing as a general skill of multi-tasking. We can talk with a friend while driving down a familiar route under normal circumstances. If the rain comes down or we drive onto an unfamiliar route, our conversation slows down or stops altogether so that we can focus on the current situation.

Really getting real things may mean, paradoxically, doing one thing (one task involving significant cognitive effort) at a time and taking steps to reduce the likelihood of interruption and the need to switch tasks. Block out time; set expectations. When interruptions and the need to switch tasks can't be avoided we can reduce associated costs by establishing simple, "at hand" methods for quickly recording thoughts and to-dos. And we can structure tasks so that the time to resume an interrupted task is minimized. Also, we can look for "win/win" ways to "kill two birds with one stone." This is not multi-tasking. Rather, in one activity, we are accomplishing two or more goals.

Will the palmtop do it all? This chapter has followed two trends into the future by simple extrapolation. Our physical and digital worlds will merge. We will (already are) more or less constantly connected. A third trend would have us abandoning our laptops for our palmtops in the same way that we (many of us) have mostly abandoned our desktop computers for our laptops. Given adequate support for input and output (e.g., "docking" support from peripherals) there is no reason a convergence to the palmtop as our primary computing device) won't happen.

Even so, we will continue to engage in two distinct modes of information interaction:

In a "stand-up" mode, information interactions are brief, narrowly focused, event-driven and with emphasis on fast finding (look-up) and quick keeping (quick capture). Stand-up work is often, but not necessarily, done standing up. More important, stand-up work is done through the day as needed and in very short periods of time. Stand-up work is about completing a plan and referencing the information needed to do so. Refer to the travel itinerary or the address of the hotel. Present the presentation. Review the document.

In a "sit-down" mode, information interactions are broader in focus, encompassing larger sets of information and with aims defined not by immediate events but rather by anticipated (desired) future circumstance and by deeper needs—the need to understand or make sense of things, for example, before taking action or committing resources. Sit-down work is generally done during quieter periods in a day (e.g., at the beginning, end or during meeting-free intervals) when we're not likely to be interrupted. Sit-down work often involves composition, planning, and preparation. Plan a trip; compose a document; prepare a presentation.

People are observed, for example, to create information resources (e.g., lists) at a "base" (home or work office) and then to take this information with them for reference as a task (e.g., buying groceries) is completed[161]. For the palmtop to become primary, it must (with the support of peripherals) be able to support both modes.

[92] See http://en.wikipedia.org/wiki/Smartphone, http://en.wikipedia.org/wiki/Handheld_PC, http://en.wikipedia.org/wiki/PDA.

[93] Occupying a region between laptops and palmtops are tablet devices such as the Kindle and the iPad.

[94] For discussions of social affordances, see Bradner, E. (2001) and Gaver, W. (1996). For more general discussions of capabilities afforded by artifacts and their designs, see Gaver, W. (1991), MacLean et al. (1989), Carroll and Kellogg (1989) and also Norman, D. (1988).

[95] Van House et al. (2005); Abiteboul et al. (2003).

[96] For more explorations into time- and location-based retrieval and notification from a palmtop see Church and Smyth (2008). Ludford et al. (2006) and Espinoza et al. (2001).

[97] Van House et al. (2005).

[98] Multimedia presentations can now be created and edited directly on the palmtop Jokela et al. (2008).

[99] See the Wikipedia article on "Geosocial networking" (http://en.wikipedia.org/wiki/Geosocial_networking).

[100] See the Wired Magazine article, "Inside Foursquare" (http://www.wired.com/epicenter/2010/05/inside-foursquare-checking-in-before-the-party-started-part-i/, http://www.wired.com/epicenter/2010/05/inside-foursquare-checking-in-before-the-party-started-part-ii/).

[101] RFID tags are now small enough to fit on the backs of ants (http://news.bbc.co.uk/2/hi/uk_news/england/bristol/somerset/8011998.stm). For basic explanations of RFID, try http://electronics.howstuffworks.com/gadgets/high-tech-gadgets/rfid.htm ("How RFID works") or http://www.explania.com/en/animations/detail/what-is-rfid ("What is RFID?"). For a more thorough description, try the Wikipedia article on RFID (http://en.wikipedia.org/wiki/Radio-frequency_identification).

[102] A simple pairing of search terms <palmtop device> + "remote" yields many matches in a search service like Google, Bing or Yahoo. A sampling of results is listed here but the reader is advised to "refresh" the search. For the iPhone: http://www.iphone-remotes.com/Welcome.html, http://www.l5remote.com/, http://www.apple.com/itunes/remote/. For the Android: http://lifehacker.com/5709967/the-best-remote-apps-for-your-android, http://www.wired.com/gadgetlab/2009/11/5-nifty-remote-apps/, https://thinkflood.com/. For the Windows Phone: http://www.freewarepocketpc.net/ppc-tag-remote.html, http://wp7remoteapp.com/, http://gigaom.com/mobile/windows-phone-is-an-xbox-360-video-remote-control/.

[103] For entry points for information concerning Bluetooth and NFC see: http://en.wikipedia.org/wiki/Bluetooth and http://en.wikipedia.org/wiki/Near_field_communication.

[104] Search on the Web with the phrase "dictation services" and a number of Web-based services support an option to speak into a palmtop (or any telephone for that matter) and get back a written transcription shortly thereafter: http://speakwrite.com/Web/, http://wescribeit.com/, http://www.worldwidedictation.com/.

[105] For a review of projected keyboards with possible use in connection with a palmtop see, http://www.alpern.org/Weblog/stories/2003/01/09/projectionKeyboards.html.

[106] For an exploration of projected displays and their potential use on a mobile device (laptop) in support of group work see Kane et al. (2009).

[107] Change in palmtop content can also be incrementally and opportunistically backed up to the Web throughout the day as afforded by internet connectivity.

[108] Jones, W. (2007), "Keeping Found Things Found."

[109] Measurements made on the watch-watch and analyzed on the palmtop might form the basis of a palmtop-initiated emergency call—e.g., in cases where heart rate or blood pressure is far outside the normal range.

[110] http://en.wikipedia.org/wiki/Dick_Tracy.

[111] http://www.engadget.com/2010/06/04/sony-demonstrates-eye-tracking-glasses-designed-forlifelogging/.

[112] http://research.microsoft.com/en-us/um/cambridge/projects/sensecam/; http://en.wikipedia.org/wiki/Microsoft_SenseCam.

[113] NASA, for example, is experimenting with detection of subvocal speech (http://www.nasa.gov/centers/ames/news/releases/2004/subvocal/subvocal.html).

[114] Users lack "understanding of important privacy risks" and "use incomplete protective practices" while on Wi-FI Klasnja et al. (2009).

[115] For a discussion on subtle tradeoffs between a desire to share and a desire to protect privacy concerning matters of location and especially concerning one's children, see Ahern et al. (2007).

[116] O'Hara and Shadbolt (2008). Allen (2008). Brin (1999).

[117] See, for example, AOL Civil Subpoena Policy, http://legal.Web.aol.com/aol/aolpol/clvllsubpoena.html, http://communications-media.lawyers.com/privacy-law/Cell-Phone-Privacy.html.

[118] As storage gets cheaper companies may extend the period in which they keep text messages as backup. http://ask.metafilter.com/117139/Does-the-phone-company-store-your-text-messages. Data may be kept, "just in case."

http://wiki.answers.com/Q/How_do_you_subpoena_a_cellphone_provider_to_obtain_text_messages.

[119]See, for example, Coughlin (2007). http://blog.nj.com/digitallife/2007/10/tracking_himself_so_the_fbi_wo.html *Sousveillance: Inventing and Using Wearable Computing Devices for Data Collection in Surveillance Environments, Surveillance & Society.* O'Hara et al. (2008). http://www.springerlink.com/content/r273l7321v8h85t7/.

[120]IPTO (2003). Lifelog Proposer Information Pamphlet, Defense Advanced Research Projects Agency Information Processing Technology Office document PIP_03-30. http://Web.archive.org/Web/20030603173339/, http://www.darpa.mil/ipto/Solicitations/PIP_03-30.html (This is an archived version of the document. The official version of the document has been taken offline by DARPA.)

[121]For more on MyLIfebits, see http://research.microsoft.com/en-us/projects/mylifebits/default.aspx and articles by Gemmell et al. (2006, 2002, 2003).

[122]For more on CARPE: http://www.sigmm.org/Members/jgemmell/CARPE.

[123]For more on EyeTap and "wearable computing," see Mann et al. (2004), Mann and Niedzviecki (2001).

[124]http://www.nesc.ac.uk/esi/events/Grand_Challenges/proposals.

[125]See Bell, G. (2001), Bell et al. (2004), Bell and Gemmell (2009), and Czerwinski et al. (2006).

[126]For discussions on the complementarity between physical and digital memory, see Jones, W. (1986a,b, 1988), Kalnikaité and Whittaker (2007, 2008), Sellen and Whittaker (2010), Sellen et al. (2007).

[127]Bell and Gemmell (2009).

[128](p. 73).

[129]Hafner, K. (2004).

[130]Loftus, E. (1993).

[131]Jones et al. (2003).

[132]Kalnikaité and Whittaker (2007).

[133]Lansdale and Edmonds (1992).

[134]Fertig et al. (1996), Freeman and Gelernter (1996).

[135]For example, see Czerwinski and Horvitz (2002).

[136]Buckland, M. (1997).

[137]http://en.wikipedia.org/wiki/Resource_Description_Framework; http://www.w3.org/RDF/.

[138]Weitzner, D. (2007).

[139]The actions—the verbs of event statements—can be finer-grained but not usefully so without limit. For events recording our interactions with digital information, the press of a key or the click of the mouse is likely a limit of granularity. Above this level, are the "undoable" actions recorded in an application like MS Word.

[140]For discussion of a multi-tool approach to management of structure, see Jones, W. (2011) and Jones and Anderson (2011). *XES* (eXtensible Event Stream) is one proposed standard for event logging (see http://www.xes-standard.org/, http://www.xes-standard.org/_media/xes/xes_standard_proposal.pdf). Events logged via XES can be analyzed using the open source software (OSS) tool ProM (http://www.processmining.org/prom/start).

[141]One useful variation based upon our experiences with the prototyping of Planz is to record events as a kind of two-step between people and their informational environment. An event involving a person and her environment is represented in two distinct parts—intention (input to the system) and outcome (output from the system). A person clicks on a hyperlink with the intention—as desired outcome—that the page is displayed in a window (or a "tab") of the browser. But other outcomes are also possible such as the "404 error" indicating that the referenced page no longer exists. Or, to give another example, the person attempts to "delete" a local file, only to receive an error to the effect that the file is open and must be closed first.

[142]See, for example, QuickSilver (http://en.wikipedia.org/wiki/Quicksilver_(software), http://qsapp.com/) and other "application launchers" (http://en.wikipedia.org/wiki/Comparison_of_application_launchers).

[143]A Web search using terms such as "self-trackers" and "quantified self " yields a wealth of articles including (as of 1/13/2012) the following: http://www.kk.org/quantifiedself/2008/09/selftrackers.php, http://www.quantifiedself.com/, http://www.nytimes.com/2010/05/02/magazine/02self-measurement-t.html?pagewanted=all.

[144]http://en.wikipedia.org/wiki/Know_thyself, http://en.wikiquote.org/wiki/Socrates.

[145]For example, UbiFit works with a mobile device to display a "garden" that grows and blooms as we exercise (Consolvo et al., 2009, 2008).

[146]Dabbish et al. (2011), Jin and Dabbish (2009).

[147]For popular press articles on multi-tasking, see: *Slow Down, Brave Multitasker, and Don't Read This in Traffic* (http://www.nytimes.com/2007/03/25/business/25multi.html); *The Myth of Multitasking* (http://www.thenewatlantis.com/publications/the-myth-of-multitasking) and *Hooked on Gadgets, and Paying a Mental Price* (http://www.nytimes.com/2010/06/07/technology/07brain.html?

pagewanted=1&_r=1&hp). See also,
http://en.wikipedia.org/wiki/Human_multitasking#cite_note-Wallis-2.

[148]James Gleick wrote in his 1999 book *Faster*. "We are multitasking connoisseurs—experts in crowding, pressing, packing and overlapping distinct activities in our all-too-finite moments."

[149]Mark et al. (2005), Czerwinski et al. (2004), González and Mark (2004).

[150]See also Salvucci et al. (2009) for discussions of a "unified theory" of multi-tasking.

[151]Adamczyk and Bailey (2004), Iqbal and Horvitz (2007), Mark et al. (2008).

[152]For research on automaticity, see Shiffrin, R. M. and Dumais, S. T. (1981). "The development of automatism." (In J. R. Anderson (Ed.), *Cognitive skills and their acquisition* (pp. 111–140). Hillsdale, NJ: Erlbaum.) Shiffrin, R. M. and Schneider, W. (1977). "Controlled and automatic human information processing: II. Perceptual learning, automatic attending, and a general theory." *Psychological Review, 84*, 127–190.

[153]With practice, a task can become "automated." However, there is still some residual demand on mental capacity limiting our ability to do another task at the same time.

[154]In fact, people with more practice at task switching may do worse (Ophir et al., 2009).

[155]In studies of dual-task performance, there is a measurable pause in the switch from one task to the next (correlated with an, observable shift in brain activity as detected, for example, by fMRI tests). For more on neural physiological correlates to task switching see:
Slagter et al. (2007). fMRI evidence for both generalized and specialized components of attentional control. *Brain Research, 1177*, 90-102.
Slagter et al. (2006). Brain regions activated by endogenous preparatory set-shifting as revealed by fMRI. *Cognitive, Affective, and Behavioral Neuroscience*, 6, 175–189.
Buschman TJ, Miller EK. Serial, covert shifts of attention during visual search are reflected by the frontal eye fields and correlated with population oscillations. *Neuron*. 2009 Aug 13;63(3):386–96.
Rubinstein et al. (2001). Executive Control of Cognitive Processes in Task Switching. *Journal of Experimental Psychology: Human Perception and Performance*, 27 (4).

[156]Although younger people report more multi-tasking, the basic limitations in multi-tasking are shared across generations. Carrier, L. et al. (2009).

[157]Even apparently simple tasks can compete with each other (Pashler, H., 1994).

[158]Adamczyk and Bailey (2004), Cutrell et al. (2001), Czerwinski et al. (2004), Gillie and Broadbent (1989), Mark et al. (2008).

[159]See Rice, Edward (1990). *Captain Sir Richard Francis Burton: The Secret Agent Who Made the Pilgrimage to Makkah, Discovered the Kama Sutra,* and *Brought the Arabian Nights to the West.* New York: Charles Scribner's Sons.

[160]Carrier, L. et al. (2009).

[161]Ludford et al. (2006).

CHAPTER 4

Our Information, Forever on the Web

One measure of the Web's importance is to imagine what life would be without it. Those of us who are older have lived in a world without the Web. Think back. How did we buy and sell stocks? Did we really call a broker on the phone? Likewise, did we call to get directions to a new restaurant, writing these down as delivered by a person on the other end? Or, when planning a vacation, did we send away for brochures? Did we wait days or weeks only to find out that the information delivered was not what we wanted? Today "it's on the Web." Retrieval is interactive; results come back in seconds. Word definitions, health information, weather reports, news headlines, stock prices, and deals on just about everything—it's all on the Web.

What is the Web vs. the Internet? The Internet through the standard Internet Protocol Suite (TCP/IP)[162] is a global "network of networks," interconnecting computers and storage, processing power and data, worldwide. Strictly speaking, the Web is only a part of the Internet[163]. Information items, in the form of hypermedia Web pages, are represented for display in a wide range of Web browsers using a markup language such as HTML or XHTML. Pages are addressed and interconnected via Uniform Resource Locators (URLs) or, more generally, Uniform Resource Identifiers (URIs)[164].

Some argue that use of the Web is in decline in favor of special-purpose applications (i.e., those of a palmtop device like an iPhone, Windows or Android phone) that use the

Internet without using the Web[165]. We note, however, that these arguments as well as the hundreds of responses to these articles are posted—where else?—on the Web. The Web is often where we first learn about the special-purpose applications for our mobile devices. The Web is where we go to exchange information about these applications. The Web is the visible "face" of the Internet. In common parlance, "Web" and "Internet" are often used interchangeably. This chapter will do so as well. The Web will stand for the larger Internet, unless otherwise noted.

This chapter complements Chapter 3. Our Information. Always and Forever. Always at hand, thanks to our palmtop devices. But there is nothing "forever" about these devices or the information we keep on them. Devices break. They are lost or stolen. Or they are discarded in favor of newer models.

By contrast, the Web is a place where information persists. Nothing, of course, is forever. But we can—and should—be thinking of information management over a longer, indefinite period of time. Our information can, potentially, persist for decades on the Web. Our information can outlive us, becoming a part of our legacy. If we are nomadic as we use our palmtops then the Web is where we might settle down. The Web is even where we might achieve a measure of immortality.

Our information as a "thing" also changes state as we move from the mobile, peripatetic uses of information in the last chapter to a consideration of the Web as a place where information persists. Information discussed in the last chapter was liquid—"data in motion"[166], a stream channeled through various applications and services, moving over, under and through us during our day and from us on to other people.

Our information on the Web becomes a thing to be addressed (via URI), linked to, organized and placed into larger contexts. Pictures posted and inter-linked tell the story of a summer vacation. Presentations, papers and statements of research project interlinked through a Web-based resume tell the story of a career. Construction drawings, site pictures, emails, bills received and paid, etc. tell the story of a house re-model. Our information on the Web begins to take shape and to have a structure. Our information on the Web is more solid than liquid.

Consider the differences between information as a liquid and information as a solid.

1. **Information as a liquid** flows from sender to recipient and through a course of tools—services, applications and devices. We direct, divert and even "dam" but with limited success. We don't control liquid information any more than we control the water running through our fingers. The email, text, tweet or photo is out of our control as soon as we post it. We do little to curate or structure liquid information.

2. **Information as a solid** has place and position. We can encourage the construction of roads to our information through the content and links we select for our web presences, our selection of metatags, descriptive URLs and our choices in other forms of search engine optimization (SEO)[167]. We might also begin to invest in walls to protect the more personal areas of our web presence from scrutiny by the general public. Flimsy ones can be built through the use of robots.txt or through choices in privacy settings supported by service providers like Facebook. Stronger walls can be built through uses of encryption and secured access. When information stays put and holds its shape, there are good reasons to structure. There are good reasons to build both roads and walls.

As our information grows and takes shape on the Web, we need tools of a different kind. We need tools that can be applied to our information—its content and structure—where and as it is. It is no longer acceptable that our information (through export and import utilities) should move from tool to tool and (necessarily) change its shape to accommodate the current tool. Export/import becomes too troublesome and there is too much chance for loss—either loss of content and structure in the information being transferred or, certainly, a loss of context as this information is detached from the whole.

Think of a house as a metaphor for our information on the Web. The house sometimes needs repair—pipes can leak, circuits can short, heaters can fail. But the tools needed for repair (and the people who know how to use these tools) come to the house not vice versa. Likewise, as we consider a re-model to add a home office or a guest bedroom, we don't tear the house down to build from scratch. Rather we build upon an existing structure. Moreover, we would think it a crazy world if our desire to switch from one plumber, electrician or contractor to the next meant that we must switch houses too.

But then notice something. By the house metaphor for our information on the Web, most of us are renting apartments. Or we're guests who might be turned out of our host's home at any time. Worse, we're guests at the homes of several hosts—we sleep at the home of one host; watch TV at the home of another; and use the kitchen at the home of another host. If an outlet doesn't work, we don't have a choice of electricians. Instead, we depend upon the choices made by our superintendent or host. (Perhaps we must work with the ne're-do-well brother-in-law who would otherwise be unemployed.) Re-modeling is obviously out of the question.

But does it really make sense for us to settle down on the Web? After all, home ownership in the real world comes with a host of headaches and responsibilities. What would "settling down" on the Web look like? And what compensatory benefits does it bring for the added responsibility? How will the Web change to accommodate us as home owners rather than guests or renters? And why might we decide to "own?" This chapter explores these questions in two sections.

1. **Read, write … realize!** The Web evolves and updates itself everywhere, continuously, in a million small ways with each passing minute. But to make sense of the Web we impose a fiction—the desktop notion of "releases." "Web 2.0" marks an increasing focus on the social and the use of the web to talk back via blogs, wikis, tweets, the posts to Facebook "walls" and so on. What then would a "Web 3.0" represent? Many answers are possible. From a practical PIM standpoint, one answer makes special sense—the Web is a place we go to make things happen.

2. **Living on the Web**. We're doing more and more things on the Web or through the Internet-enabled applications of our devices. As we use the Web, how is the web affecting us? How can we use the Web to live the lives we want to live?

4.1 READ, WRITE, … REALIZE!

What is the future of the Web? What is Web 3.0? If we look, here are some of the answers we'll find.

- **A smarter Web.** The Web will be "semantic"[168] with data represented in machine-readable form using a language such as RDF or XML.to create a "Web of data"[169].

- **A more physical Web**. Chapter 3 considered a "more digital" world in which the information gained from our five senses is augmented by digital information available from the Web. (What restaurants are nearby? Who is that person over in the corner?). Conversely, navigation through the Web can become a more physical experience. Think *Second Life* or the gestural affordances of Kinect only applied across the Web. The Web becomes a virtual world in which we can walk and gesture nearly as we can in our physical world[170]. The Web together with our devices might then form a "metaverse" that merges the physical and the digital[171].

In more prosaic, practical visions, a future Web will provide[172].

1. "Micropayments for quality content."

2. "Interactive magazines in a more interactive format (including options to "talk back" via blog comments, wikis and tweets)."

3. "(Even more) collaborative and real-time content."

4. "Better Web security against phishing, scams and spam."

5. "An on-line operating system (OS)."

6. "Customized user interfaces."

7. ...

And so on.

The future is a moving target. Some items on future lists are already here. Think, for example, of Amazon's very successful model for "micro"—or perhaps "mini"—payments in connection with content delivered to a Kindle. Some items, such as the semantic web, are harder to define and seem forever on a receding horizon.

How to shape a discussion of the future of the Web in ways so that we can understand its relevance and without pointing to signposts that will quickly recede into a rearview window? And what about the forks in our road into the future? Do we have choices other than (with apologies to Yogi Berra[173]) simply to "take it," i.e., can we influence the direction taken into a future Web?

4.1.1 A PROGRESSION

Consider the more commonly noted differences between "Web 1.0" and "Web 2.0." Anderson, P. (2007) lists key ideas behind the Web 2.0 which include support for individual production and user generated content, the ability to harness the power of the crowd, data on a very large "epic" scale, greater openness and an "architecture of participation."

Cormode and Krishnamurthy (2008) noted that "the essential difference between Web 1.0 and Web 2.0 is that content creators were few in Web 1.0 with the vast majority of users simply acting as consumers of content, while any participant can be a content creator in Web 2.0."

The Web initially, for most of us, was a one-way, read-only experience. Now communication on the Web is two-way. We tag; we blog and we author wikis. We post photographs, videos and reviews. In an age of Web 2.0, we write as well as read.

A progression towards a Web 3.0 is then suggested by the "chmod" (for "change mode")[174] command of the venerable Unix system. For a given file or folder, chmod is used to set permissions to read, write and ... execute a file. Executable files represent the tools (utilities, applications) that people can run to get things done.

Or we might say "Read, wRite, Run"—call these the three "R's" of computing[175]. If a Web 1.0 was mostly about reading information from the Web and a Web 2.0 provides much wider support for writing back to the Web, then a Web 3.0 might be about running our computing applications *on* the Web or *through* a Web browser.

But "execute" has wider meanings of relevance to PIM—execute as in "to carry out; to put into effect"[176]. Read, write and then ***realize***.

Get things done. Make things happen—not in a simulated reality on the Web itself but in the real lives we wish to live. Let this be the theme for a Web 3.0 of great potential relevance to each of us. The Web is a grand place of convergence for all the resources we need—data, programming and computation, the time and expertise of other people[177]—in order to effect useful change in our material lives.

By this reckoning, the leading edge of Web 3.0 has long since arrived. Just as we could write to the Web years before anyone spoke of a "Web 2.0," we have long been able to run applications on the Web. Those of us inclined toward programming can choose from a variety of programming languages, utilities and services specifically designed to support creation of the executable code that runs on the Web.

We also turn increasingly to the Web to *realize,* i.e., to make things happen. Reservations for plane, train, hotel and restaurant are all made through the Web. We expect these to turn into the reality of a seat, a room or a table, respectively. Flowers arrive at the bedside of a loved one convalescing in the hospital—an outcome of a complex chain of events set in motion by us with a few clicks or presses of our thumbs. We order and download digital music or films for immediate enjoyment. We use our current palmtop or laptop with Web connection to order its replacement—confident this new device will "materialize" a few days later. With developments in 3-D printing, the day may not be far away when physical objects too can materialize in our home or office only a matter of minutes after their order on the Web[178].

As already discussed in Chapter 3, there are still more possibilities to be realized through a combined use of the Web and a palmtop device[179]. For example, we text for concert tickets and priority passes to amusement parks. Our pass or proof of purchase can be displayed directly from the palmtop for a ticket agent to see—no need for paper.

Our efforts to make things happen through the Web are made easier because information about us—our names, addresses and credit card numbers, our preferences (for window vs. aisle seat)—persists (securely we hope) on-line so that the incremental time to initiate a new transaction is minimal. How much more might we realize as more of "us" is on-line? As we become home-owners on the Web perhaps we can expect a home delivery of information so that we no longer need to go shopping from Web site to Web site to order the things we want for our physical world.

One room of our house—an outer room, a parlor room—might include our plans for a special night on the town. We describe the night we have in mind. When? Where? (What part of town?) For how many? What kind of restaurant? What kind of film or show? Vendors come to us, leaving their calling cards and their offers. At our leisure, we select the offer that most closely matches the evening we have in mind. Another room of the house might describe our dreams for a summer vacation in Paris with a similar opportunity for vendors to leave their best offers for our consideration. Fantasy now; but very possibly real sometime soon[180].

In the meantime, the reality for many of us is still anchored in desktop applications—i.e., applications installed on a desktop or laptop computer. Three preceded the Web and have changed very little in their basic purpose even as their usefulness and usability have dramatically improved through a succession of releases over three decades: a word-processing application is for making text-mostly documents, a spreadsheet application is for analyzing and presenting numerical data, a presentation-maker application is for making visual slides in support of oral presentations.

More recent additions to this application troika include the Web browser (we may switch between several), a multi-purpose email/calendar/contact/task-management "PIM" application, a viewer for reading and possibly editing documents published in PDF format and possibly a few additional applications specific to our profession or place of work[181].

Many of these applications are packaged into a "suite" of applications. By far the most commonly used is Microsoft Office[182]. As a Web 3.0 is more fully realized over the next few years, will we still be using Microsoft Office? Will we still be using "everything" applications—Web-enabled to be sure but still large and monolithic? Or will we be working in a much wider space of smaller, specialized, "mix & match" tools that we can use in various combinations according to our needs and goals? Do we have reason to care one way or the other? And, if so, can we have influence on the Web's future direction?

The best one-word answer to each of the questions above is "yes." Questions are more properly explored in the following sub-sections.

From the desktop to the Web and back again. Desktop applications are becoming more Web-like and Web sites/services are becoming more like desktop applications. A meeting in the middle will likely take the form of hybrids with a client/server synthesis of functionality: Device-local processing of data for matters relating to us and our physical situation; remote processing and data (on any of a number of servers) for matters relating to other people and the shared objects of our collaboration.

Moving on out: From vertical high-rises to bands of horizontal integration. Our larger desktop applications provide a great many services in support of a "soup to nuts" creation of information items such as documents, financial analyses and presentations. But performance with a given service—document version comparison, for example, or slide layout—may be far from ideal. Likewise, some Web-based applications position themselves as "everything buckets"[183] for our information. These applications offer a variety of services including information capture, storage, synchronization between our devices, notifications and even OCR. A better future gives us ways to break apart the structure of these vertically integrated applications so that we can pick and choose those tools best suited to our needs. As we do this we can begin to realize bands of horizontal integration in accordance with basic activities of PIM such as keeping and refinding, which must be done for all our information items no matter whether their form is called a "document," "presentation," "spreadsheet," "task" or "note."

The objects of our application, Part I[184]: Towards modular units of construction. Finally, we consider the potential of a basic form of item which might serve as a modular unit in our efforts to build our digital houses of information.

4.1.2 FROM THE DESKTOP TO THE WEB AND BACK AGAIN

First, consider the larger "desktop" applications—i.e., applications that are installed and run (mostly) on a local device (a desktop, laptop or, even, a palmtop computer). The more commonly used of these are packaged into "office suites"[185] such as Microsoft Office[186]. MS Office bundles together the applications of Microsoft Word, Microsoft Excel and Microsoft PowerPoint to support the creation of documents, spreadsheets, and presentations, respectively. MS Office also includes Microsoft Outlook as combined provider of email, task, calendar and contact management. Apache OpenOffice[187] packages applications that also provide for the creation of documents, spreadsheets and presentations (Writer, Calc and Impress, respectively).

Desktop applications in support of the creation of documents, spreadsheets and presentations are large—even monolithic. So too is a PIM manager like MS Outlook. Later, we'll consider whether the objects of these applications are really the "thing" anymore. If our "object" (our objective) is to communicate, explain, persuade or analyze, does the Web now provide us with better alternatives?

Here we note that these applications have changed over the years to take advantage of the Web. User assistance (help) increasingly defaults to on-line access. Help comes on-line via supporting documentation, videos, email exchanges and interactive chats. We turn to the Web also for various application templates (e.g., presentation color schemes, letter samples, spreadsheet business plans) and for the support and suggestions of user groups. Updates and new releases too are increasingly distributed through the Web.

Even if our primary applications are still rooted ("installed") to our computing devices, therefore, an increasing number of associated services are moving to and realized through the Web. Will our applications themselves follow?

The potential ...and the limitations ...of the Web-based applications

Moving to the Web has many advantages. Graham, P. (2001) noted that web-based applications and services run to the benefit of both the consumer and the provider. Consider, for example, a Web-based email service. People can access their email accounts from any computer or palmtop device via any Web browser. Application and user data too (email messages, calendar appointments, contact information) are on-line for "anywhere access." The email service can be constantly, seamlessly "upgraded." The user doesn't need to download a new release. There is no need to "restart" the computer.

Moreover, Web access greatly increases the range of potentially useful applications and the timeliness of their access. Under a Software as a Service (SaaS) model[188] we might pay "a la carte" for "just in time" access to the software needed for the task at hand.

Conversely, developers get immediate feedback concerning the success or failure of a new design. Not sure which variation of a feature to use? Try each on a random sampling of users and assess their relative merits through immediate observation of the feature's actual use. Problems in an application, ranging from outright bugs to more subtle problems of design are more quickly observed and fixes to these more easily deployed.

Companies like Google, whose origins are Web-based, may be in an especially strong position to challenge the desktop application model of software tools with Web-based alternatives[189]. But Microsoft is countering with an Office 365[190] which offers different options for Office applications: 1. Run locally but Web-enabled to realize updating and collaborative features; or 2. Run completely Web-based[191].

But how good are Web-based applications? In an ideal, users of *rich internet applications*[192] experience nearly the same interactivity as for desktop applications running locally. In actual comparisons to their desktop counterparts, Web-based applications are still apt to be slower, less interactive and with fewer UI constructs (e.g., "drag & drop")[193].

At the same time, Web sites are working more like applications

Already and now especially with the arrival of HTML 5.0[194], Web sites in general are becoming more interactive so that the boundary between Web-based applications and ordinary Web pages is blurred. The information on a page may change dynamically (sometimes with no need for a round-trip to the Web site server) as boxes are checked, buttons clicked, and drop-down choices made. Users have less need to "go" somewhere—a new page or a new site altogether—in order to get the information they need. Information "comes" to the user instead[195].

Even if user input prompts a wholesale regeneration of the Web page, this "get" can be done in ways that preserve the essential structure and context of the Web page so that the transition to the display of new information is less disruptive[196]. As one indication that sites are becoming more interactive, people are making much less use of the "back" button of the Web browser[197]. Web sites and services such as gmail and Facebook become places that we visit and "live in" for extended periods of time much as we do with the conventional word processor or email client application of the desktop.

Increasing the application-like behavior of Web sites carries obvious benefits for the Web site provider. Users who stray from a Web page in a search for needed information may leave the Web site altogether; users who stay on a page, stay on the site (and its advertisements). Benefits may accrue for users too. Users who can stay on a page to complete a transaction will certainly experience fewer distractions and may even have the experience that the transaction is completed more quickly[198].

We can expect that Web-based applications will continue to improve[199] to be faster and more interactive in the manner of desktop applications. In the other direction, a steadily increasing number of the components in desktop applications will find their way onto the Web for ease of updating and everywhere access. Movements in both directions will converge on hybrid meetings in the middle that take the form of client/server syntheses of functionality: Device-local processing of data for matters relating to us and our physical situation; remote processing and data (on any of a number of servers) for matters relating to other people and the shared objects of our collaboration.

4.1.3 MOVING ON OUT: FROM VERTICAL HIGH-RISES TO BANDS OF HORIZONTAL INTEGRATION

Whether the applications and services we use still run mostly on our devices or on the Web or in some happy combination of both, these still function very much as worlds unto themselves. We have a limited freedom (rarely exercised by the average user) to customize settings for matters such as sharing and privacy. Applications can sometimes be usefully extended through an inclusion of plug-ins, a use of macro programming languages (such as VBA[200]) and through other tools that work through the application supported API.

Applications such as MS Word and Web-based services such as Facebook differ in many respects but they share a common focus on "soup-to-nuts,"[201] start-to-finish vertical integration[202] of function—in the one case, towards completion of a document and, in the second case, towards a realization of social networking.

In a world of vertically integrated applications and services, who really owns our information? Are we home owners, renters or guests? With respect to Web-based services such as Facebook (or Gmail, YouTube, Flickr, etc.) we are guests. These services include storage management in their package of vertically-integrated functions. But it is their storage, not ours. We have limited control over the information we post. The control we do choose to exercise (e.g., privacy settings) is uncertain and not easily verified[203]. Our information might be lost temporarily or even permanently[204]. Services may shutdown[205].

We may feel a greater sense of ownership and control over the information we create through applications (such as MS Word) that package this information into files we can save to our device-local file system. We can, after all, move these files from place to place and we can copy them to back-up. Even where there is a mapping to storage on a device we own, however, we have considerably less control than we might wish for. For example, the information we wish to work with does not always neatly align with file-level items such as "documents," "presentations" or "spreadsheets." We often wish to work with smaller units of information as structured within a larger unit. Perhaps we want to access a paragraph of disclaimer text within a larger file-level document or a graphic within a larger presentation. In these and other cases, we are forced to go through the "owning" application.

Vertical integration can be a good thing. As we work to complete a conventional document in printed form, for example, we may go through distinct phases from brainstorming and idea generation to finer-grained formatting and "wordsmithing" to spell-checking and then on to a review prior to print-out or posting. Each stage calls for its own set of tools—mind-mapping and outlining, for the first phase, conventional word-processing for the second stage and tools for spelling and grammar checking for the third phase. We want these tools to work well together.

But large, vertically integrated applications can be a bad thing. Call them "monoliths."[206] Monoliths build in a great many functions related to particular activity (such as document processing, task management, or social networking). Functions can sometimes work together beautifully in support of the user, but not always. Only a very small percentage of the features in an application like MS Word are used by the average person[207]. Worse, the sheer number of features, taken together, can confuse and obfuscate. Features often interact in unexpected and perplexing ways (even to those charged with application testing and development). And, with respect to the functions that we actually use, we may find ourselves stuck with only one, hard-to-use way of doing something badly (think outlining or styles in MS Word) when we might wish for a free-market choice between several competing ways of accomplishing a function. We may in fact think that functions of a monolith are little better integrated than the various implements of a massive Swiss army knife (see Figure 4.1).

Figure 4.1: Are the functions of a monolith like the instruments of an extremely large Swiss army knife?[208]

People don't simply dislike monoliths. They hate them. Why? On a search service of your choice, use the pattern "I hate ..." and put in the name of the application in question. You'll find an abundance of web pages—many crackpot but many others listing legitimate grievances[209]. The vehemence expressed is more than anything else a product of a sense of powerlessness and a sense that there is no choice—people are struck with what they have. Monoliths are, so to speak, the applications people "hate to use every day."

Can useful integrations be accomplished in ways that don't force us to use monoliths? And what about other forms of integration? Why not, for example, an integration what would allow us to capture (create, copy, take) a useful graphic or picture together with an explanatory textual caption (possibly delivered initially via voice or generated through OCR) and then to use the information item so created in several different ways? The item might have use as a figure in a document and also as a slide (with the caption as a speaker note) in a presentation and possibly also as a photograph in a digital photo album or a scrapbook.

There is obvious integration in this example. But it is a different kind of integration from those we've discussed in the context of the creation of a document, presentation or a social networking web presence. Call it *horizontal integration*[210] since integration cuts across the information forms and activities defined by the monoliths.

Horizontal vs. vertical approaches to integration are nicely contrasted through a consideration of three genres of application.

- **Reference managers** support the collection, organization, sharing and citation use of bibliographic references. Example applications include the Web-based Mendeley and Zotero (and also the originally desktop-based Endnote)[211].

- **Note managers** support the capture, organization and use of notes and annotated references to other information items (esp. Web pages). Example applications include Evernote and Microsoft OneNote[212].

- **Task managers** support the capture, organization and completion of tasks and to-dos. Examples include Remember The Milk, OmniFocus and Outlook Tasks[213].

Reference managers

Students, professors and everyone who has ever written a scholarly paper have struggled with the challenge of referencing related work. In particular, how to format these references both in in-line citations and in a reference list (bibliography)? People who publish repeatedly often create their own collection of citations for papers and books they reference frequently. These references are managed by one of several applications now available for the management and formatting of references including EndNote, Mendeley and Zotero. Each application has its strengths and weaknesses[214].

As one user comments: "*I prefer zotero when I'm browsing the net and searching for papers, but I prefer a fully dedicated program like mendeley for later editing and browsing my own collection.*" And, from another user on the same discussion board: "*I don't want to be locked into using just Mendeley or Zotero*"[215].

All bibliographic applications encode the same basic set of attributes for each of the works being referenced. These include author, title, year of publication, publisher or publishing journal and so on. These attributes are described by standards such as Dublin Core[216]. Many of these bibliographic applications share information concerning variations in citation style and bibliographic formatting across different publications[217]. Several applications even use the same embedded relational database management utility, SQLite[218], as part of their back-end store.

But there is still no way (yet) for people to freely switch between applications as applied to the same database. Instead, users must export from one and import into the other. To take advantage of front-end features in each of several applications, users must manage an equal number of databases and face a likelihood of inconsistencies and incomplete conversions between these. In the face of the time, uncertainty and complexity involved in conversions form one to another application, most of us, instead, pick one application and forgo the advantages of the others.

A user expresses a hope for the development of Mendeley and Zotero that we might generalize to other bibliography reference tools: *"These 2 great projects will definitely gain strength if they can work better together, but that requires their worlds to come closer, 2 way sync of their databases and, who knows, in the future a single shared database?"*[219].

Note managers

Substitute "citations" or "bibliographic references" in discussions above with "notes," "annotations" or "captured information" and much of the same discussion still applies. A large and growing class of applications help us with the capture of information—not for formal use in bibliographic referencing, but simply so that information "found" might "stay found" for later use[220].

These applications will be referred to here as "note managers" with the understanding that the category is quite broad and that "notes" can be multi-media—text to be sure but also sound, pictures and even full-motion video. We take notes during a meeting or a talk and possibly as synched with an audio or video recording of the meeting. We take notes and excerpts—text and images—from a Web page and also from a local document. Using a headset or a special kind of watch as described in Chapter 3, we might make an audio note to capture an important thought or reminder as we walk or wait for the bus.

Two note-taking applications will help to stake a very large space in note-taking variations. MS OneNote originated as a single-user desktop application and has evolved to have support for a collaborative sharing of notes through a synchronized presence on the Web and the desktop. Evernote began as a purely Web-based note-taking application but now offers desktop versions too.

Both MS OneNote and Evernote offer "quick capture" options through integrations with other applications. Both provide ways to group, arrange, tag and otherwise organize the notes collected. OneNote users can organize notes in a two-space grouped by section tabs (top) and pages (to the right side). Evernote users can organize notes into projects with optional use of a hierarchically organized set of tags and with the ability to see filtered views based upon tag selection.

As with reference managers, we might hope for an ability to switch freely between Evernote, MS OneNote and other note managers as these are applied *to the same set of notes.* We might, for example, use MS OneNote for its support of note-taking synchronized with audio recording and then we might use Evernote, on the same set of notes, for its support of OCR of text in photos. Alas, note managers like reference managers, do not work with each other except (imperfectly) via export and import. Note managers function instead as vertically integrated monoliths (or "everything buckets")[221].

Task managers

Task managers are packaged in various ways to help with "productivity" or "to-do lists" or in support of "Getting things done." By a recent count, there were over 160 task managers designed to work with David Allen's "Getting Things Done"[222] methodology. Many are web-based[223].

Just as with bibliographic and note-taking applications, we see discussions concerning the relative merits of different task managers. For example, we read that OmniFocus (OF) is very complete but perhaps overly complex[224]. Outlook Tasks provides a folder model for organization and supports to-do reminders in a larger context of meeting and appointment reminders[225], etc.

Some might argue that the large number and diversity of task management applications is simply a reflection of the number and diversity of our task management needs as individual users[226]. If so, we could wish that it were easier to try out, switch between and mix-and-match the various applications that are available. The sense of discussion boards, instead, is that the switch from one task manager to another is a difficult, even painful, choice and not taken lightly.

Also, many of us reading this may not currently use any of the many applications specially designed for task management. Our systems of task management may, instead, be ad hoc. Perhaps we text or email notes to ourselves as a reminder of a to-do. Or perhaps we scribble reminders on a piece of paper or into a digital calendar as "appointments." For longer to-do lists, we may use a simple text document or spreadsheet. Perhaps we tried a task manager—as a separate application or as one of the utilities supported in a larger application like MS Outlook—and concluded that use of the task manager was more trouble than it was worth[227].

Our own system for managing tasks (and to-dos, appointments, etc.)—whether this involves software tools, paper notepads or is done mostly in our heads—is a product of our own trial and error explorations and is continually evolving. Even if we had a dedicated team of software developers ready to write a customized application for our specific needs, we might be hard-pressed to say what those needs are or *will be.*

How could it be easier explore and to switch from one task manager to another and what might it take for those of us "sitting on the sidelines" to give task managers a (another) try?

A basis for comparing task managers

Even as the list of task managers gets longer and longer (with each passing day, it seems), the list of task-relevant attributes is stable. Although their names may vary, we expect the attributes to describe the task with a title or short description and to establish a "due date" (and time). A higher-level task or project may contain (be decomposed into) lower-level tasks. Other attributes may establish a "begin by" date (and time), a priority, % done already, dependencies with other tasks, recurrence and status (e.g., "pending" or "completed") and assignment to other people, etc.[228].

How do task managers really differ from one another? Task managers clearly differ with respect to device coverage and platform coverage. Task managers are often specific to a platform and product line. OmniFocus, for example, runs on Macintosh computers, the iPhone, iPod Touch and iPod. Some task managers run only as desktop applications. But, increasingly, task managers work across a "form factor" range of our daily devices (e.g., palmtop, tablet, laptop/desktop). Task managers that work across several devices must then work to insure that task information is consistent and current across these devices. In addition, task managers vary with respect to the lifecycle of a task.

1. **Capture and data entry**. Task managers provide entry forms for the specification of new tasks and also for the editing of existing tasks (e.g., to change title, due date, priority or status). These forms are similar to the entry forms provided for creating notes. Task managers distinguish themselves according to the ease and accessibility their "create-task" entry forms. For some task managers, entry is only possible through the main UI of the application. Other task managers support entry from within a variety of other applications (e.g., IE, FireFox, MS Outlook) and across a range of our daily devices from laptops to palmtops. Some entry forms are cumbersome to complete; others are fast and easy to complete through mechanisms such as "auto-fill." The pop-up create-task function in some task managers is able to "read" information in the larger context (e.g., from an active Web page, document or email message) in order to provide reasonable guesses concerning task attributes.

2. **Organization and structuring**. Task managers vary with respect to the structuring they support through tagging, grouping, and the creation of higher-level objects such as lists and projects.

3. **Views for display**. Task managers provide various views of task information—tasks "due" today (i.e., where due date is today's date), tasks overdue (where due date is before today's date), tasks "to do at work" (e.g., where location or "area" is "work"), tasks "done" (e.g., where "status" is set to "completed"), "waiting

for" (where status is set to "waiting for" and "waiting for" is set to a person), and so on. Views are the "face" of a task manager. Although views may differ dramatically from one task manager to the next, all are accomplished through standard variations in filtering, column display and sorting.

4. **Notifications.** Notifications (reminders, alerts) work in a direction opposite to capture and data entry. Through notifications task managers push task information outward to the devices and applications we're likely to use in a typical day. Task information may appear, for example, in the calendar or inbox view of an application like MS Office or Google Calendar. Task managers may use device-specific facilities (such as a ringtone or a pop-up alert) in order to bring attention to a notification.

A PIM basis for horizontal integration

We can generalize further. The activities in the life cycle of a task are not that different from the activities in the life cycle of a note or a bibliographic reference. Activities correspond to the basic activities of PIM as described in Chapter 2.

1. *Capture and Keep.* Take a picture; copy a graphic or some lines of text. Label and/or place[229]; apply OCR or speech recognition for explanatory text. Specify additional attributes and tags (or "accept" inferred values for these). The event of capture and the captured item need to be plastic—we may not know initially whether the item is to be a simple note, a reference, a task, a funny message to a friend or perhaps all of these. Can we have support for capture that works comparably well for all the kinds of

information we wish to capture and across all the devices we use?

2. *Maintain and organize.* Information captured must be synchronized between our devices and backed-up (e.g., synchronized with a Web copy). In the larger context of a collection, items (tasks, notes, references) may need to be re-organized and grouped.

3. *Manage privacy and the flow of information.* We may want to share our notes and references with others— perhaps a team of people we are working with or a larger community of people who share common interests. We may want to assign tasks. As we share with some people, we may want to take steps to hide this same information from others.

4. *Measure and evaluate.* Reference, note, task ... no matter the form of information, we are often interested in answering the same questions. "Are my strategies of time management working?" "Where is my time going?" "What % of these items do I actually 'use' or complete?" And, more generally, "How (as measured through my information) am I doing?;" "How do I compare with others?"

5. *Make sense of things.* Across item types, we look for ways to answer basic questions like "What do I have here" and "What is this telling me?" For a collection of notes (or references) we might ask: "Do I have enough yet for an article (or term paper, or report)?" "Does the current organization (or plan, or outline) still make sense?" For the tasks of a project we might ask: "Does this represent a good plan?;" "Can the tasks be completed in the allotted time?"

6. *Find/re-find, remind, use/re-use.* We want fast access to a note ("that Web page I stumbled across last week") or

a reference ("The article by Whittaker and Sidner") or a task ("What is the deadline for registration again?"). We may wish to be reminded (e.g., to look at a note or to complete a task before the deadline).

4.1.4 THE OBJECTS OF OUR APPLICATIONS, PART I: UNITS AND TOOLS OF CONSTRUCTION

Which do we want—horizontal vs. vertical integration of our tools and their features? Obviously, we want a degree of both. But a shift of focus, from the vertical to the horizontal, encourages us to think in ways that cross the traditional boundaries of information form that are themselves largely a function of our current applications. Do we want to capture a simple note, a reference, a to-do/task or an epiphany? We may not always know. Why should we have to choose? Why not a flexible means of capture that just works and works across all of our daily devices? Likewise, are we searching for a document, a presentation or an email message? Sometimes we know but other times we don't. We expect (though this is relatively recent[230]) to be able to search across these and other forms of information in cases where we're not sure.

At the same time, we would not be happy to exchange one prison cell, so to speak, for another. We do not want to be locked into the use of a particular tool of information capture or a particular tool of search and sorting. Fortunately, becoming captive to a horizontally integrated tool is less likely for the simple reason that these tools need to work well with others in the "supply chain," i.e., tools focusing on support of a particular activity of PIM or a particular stage in the lifecycle of information need to work well with other tools designed to support a different PIM activity or a different lifecycle stage.

We need tools that can make house calls—that is, tools that come to our information. What we need is illustrated in two examples of horizontal integration. In the first example, we are able to pick and choose between a large number of Web-based photo editors that work with our photographs "in place." In the second example, ordinary desktop folders stay where they are but also move. These folders get a new life and utility through their synchronization across devices and through their sharing with other people. We consider each example in turn.

Web-based photo editors "mix & match" to work with out photographs in place

Many Web-based photo editors are now able to work with our photographs as is—in their current format and in their current location. Our pictures can be stored in our local file system or in storage as provided by one of several on-line services such as Facebook and Flickr. Note, therefore, that a picture stays put—in its format, in its store—to be edited first by one applications and then, if we choose, by another.

The list of these Web-based editors is long and growing: *Fauxto, Flauntr, Fotoflexer, Lunapic, Phixr, Phoenix, Photoshop.com, Picnik free, Picnik premium, Picture2Life, Pixenate, Pixer.us, Pixlr, Preloadr, PXN8, Snipshot, Snipshot Pro, Splashup*[231]. Most are free.

For the worse, the list of choices can confuse and none are likely to be as complete as an installed desktop application such as Photoshop[232]. For the better—potentially the much better—these on-line applications may collectively afford users a much more complete set of choices. Users can freely move between applications, picking and choosing according to their photo editing needs. These applications compete with each other with respect to features such as special effects, maximum resolution, support for multiple layers and overall ease of use.

Clive Thompson writes: "*This spring, ... I reformatted the hard drive. As I went about reinstalling my software, I couldn't find my Photoshop disc. I forgot about it—until a week later, when I was blogging and needed to tweak a photo. Frustrated, I went online and discovered FotoFlexer, one of several free Web-based editing tools. I uploaded my picture, and in about one minute I'd cropped it, deepened the color saturation, and sharpened it. I haven't used Photoshop since*"[233].

As another user notes, "*It used to be, I'm buying a paint program, and I'll get the one with 5,000 features. I don't know what 2,000 of those features are, but I'll get it just in case. (Today) applications are competing on merit; they're not competing on bulk*"[234].

But here the question naturally arises: If we can freely switch between different editors as we work with our photographs, then why can't we freely switch between different editors as we work with our documents, spreadsheets and presentations? MS Office documents, spreadsheets and presentations are now natively expressed using XML (with extensions docx, xlsx and pptx, respectively) making it potentially easier for other applications to work directly with the MS Office format. Indeed, other office suites, including OpenOffice[235] and SoftmakerOffice[236], now promise to not only to read but also to write to MS Office formats.

In principle then, we might leave our MS Office information items in place and apply different tools to the same item (document, spreadsheet, presentation) depending upon our needs and the current situation. Alternate office suites are considerably cheaper than MS Office (or even free), thus giving an economic incentive to try alternatives.

Alas, the success of suite alternatives is still limited and Microsoft Office remains dominant. Why? Partly because, notwithstanding intent, other applications often do not "round trip" perfectly[237]. A user who starts the journey from an MS Excel spreadsheet and into an alternate use of another spreadsheet application, for example, may find that some macros no longer work on the return to MS Excel.

Another reason for the continued dominance of the MS Office suite of applications is that these are not merely for the end user but also function as a platform for the rapid development of "macro" applications[238].

Two more basic problems are apparent: 1. the size and complexity of the objects of these applications. Documents, spreadsheets and, even presentations, are large with many interlocking pieces and many dependencies; 2. The large, vertically integrated nature of the applications. Those of us who use these applications have grown accustomed certain ways of using them. Other applications may do better with this or that feature, but, given all the features involved, matching feature for feature—not only for ease of use but for "our" use—is extremely hard to do.

Developers of alternate applications may succeed best by abandoning the vertical approach and "going horizontal" instead. As potential users (and customers),we can readily think of specific features that might be done better in a separate application. Are we frustrated with MS Word's support for a "compare and combine" of two documents? We might be willing to try the comparable feature of another application if we could be certain that the resulting document could be easily, seamlessly opened in MS Word afterwards. Or perhaps we would choose to use a "fish eye" interface[239] for the specific task of sorting a digital deck of slides, returning again to MS PowerPoint for within-slide editing after the sort is completed.

Desktop folders get new life and utility through their synchronization and sharing

For a second example of horizontal integration, we consider services that work with our desktop (device-local) folders and files to provide services of synchronization and sharing. Selected folders (and the subfolders/files within) can be synchronized with Web-storage and then to other devices. Other people can selectively be given read and write access.

Dropbox is the best known tool in this category and its popularity is due in part to the simplicity of set-up.

1. Set up an account with name and password.

2. Download and install the Dropbox tool.

3. Select a location for the Dropbox folder. Any files or folders placed in this folder are then replicated to the Dropbox web site and can be accessed via account name and password.

4. To get these files and folders to other devices (e.g., palmtops) simply install Drobox on these devices. Information is "pulled" to a device.

5. Invite another person to share a given subfolder of your Dropbox folder by specifying their email address and an optional message.

In my experience, synchronization happens in matter of seconds (given reasonable bandwidth) and sharing with others (e.g., members of geographically distributed team working on a grant proposal) is quite simple.

As a tool to in support of horizontal integration, Drobox works well but not perfectly.

1. Dropbox does synchronization and sharing simply and effectively. It works with "files" and "folders" as abstractions and does not try to provide additional features that depend, for example, upon the file format or extension. On the other hand, the security

authentication architecture of Dropbox may be inherently insecure so that the user may decide not to place personal data (e.g., about family or finances) into the Dropbox folder[240].

2. Dropbox "almost" works with our files and folders in place but not quite. Folders and files must be moved to be within the designated Dropbox folder. But the folders and files of this folder work just as they would elsewhere in our file system. We can still work with them through our file manager.

There are alternatives to Dropbox. Windows 7 supports file sharing[241] with other Windows machines on a "homegroup," "workgroup" or "domain." Other Web-based file hosting services include Box.net, FilesAnywhere, CloudMe, CrashPlan, Egnyte, iCloud, Mozy, SpiderOak, SugarSync, TitanFile, Ubuntu One, Windows Live SkyDrive, Wuala and ZumoDrive[242].

As these photo editing and folder sharing examples illustrate, horizontally integrated tools often come with two features of value to us as we build our digital houses.

1. Horizontally integrated tools are designed to do only one or a small set of things (but often across several information formats/forms and across several devices).

2. Horizontally integrated tools are able to work with our information in its current place.

These two features combine to support a reversal of the situation that holds for the monoliths. Our information can stay fixed (as a beneficiary of our "home improvement" efforts) even as our choice of tools is much more fluid.

Sometimes a Small Notion[243]

A shift from vertical to horizontal integration can work to support a more fluid mix and match of different tools applied, in place, to our information. This can work (more or less) to support a mix and match of editors applied to our photographs which stay in place. Likewise, we can continue to work with at least a subset of our files and folders (i.e., as placed within a designated folder) on a local device and, at the same time, have these files and folders synchronized for access from other devices and shared for access by other people. Here too we can choose between several services of synchronization and sharing[244].

Why not something similar for other forms of information item in our personal space of information (PSI)? We have an answer for large objects such as documents, spreadsheets and presentations which are the objects of our traditional, vertically integrated applications. Even, when these objects are stored using an open format such as XML[245] their size and the size of their originating applications represent barriers of entry. It is extremely difficult for alternate applications to match the monoliths feature for feature and, at the same time, to preserve the internal structure of the large objects involved. Even given small discrepancies in features—and certainly if information content and structure doesn't "round trip"—we scurry back to the security of the monoliths.

But what about the smaller objects we discussed previously? Reference managers, for example, each support the same conventions for formatting bibliographies and in-line citations (as mandated by the conventions of different publication styles). There is, moreover, a Dublin Core metadata initiative to standardize the description of references[246]. The Simple Dublin Core Metadata Element Set (DCMES) consists of 15 metadata elements[247] including Title, Creator, Subject, Description, Publisher, Contributor, and Date. Can't references managers like Zotero and

Mendeley simply agree on a "reference" format in the same way that photo editors each support the formats commonly used for digital photography (such as TIFF and JPEG[248])?

Similarly, most task managers support an ability to read and write in the iCalendar format for exchanging tasks and meeting requests[249]. Why not simply agree upon a format for tasks based on iCalendar? Tasks might then stay "in place" in a collection of tasks stored separately from any given tool but able to be manipulated by each[250].

Or what about notes? Note managers would need to agree upon attributes to represent the text of a note and possibly an associated picture or graphic. Possibly there should be a link to a source. And there might be information concerning the time and location of the note's "capture." How hard can this be?

There are three reasons why—even for the smaller, more modular units of information like references, notes and tasks—we've haven't seen a rush towards a greater standardization in support of a mix & match of tools applied to the information in place.

1. **Agreement concerning a standard representation**. Arriving at official standards for references, tasks, notes and other forms of information can be a painstakingly slow process.

2. **Organizing and a provision for higher-order units ("grouping items").** We notice, for example, that picture editors do not offer a mix-and-match of services for the construction of digital photo albums or newsletters. These higher-order units are still in the separate silos of vertically integrated applications and services. With respect to units we have discussed, the need for higher-order grouping items is most apparent for tasks. Tasks organized how? To do what? Remember-the-milk organizes tasks into "lists" whereas OmniFocus

uses "projects." Shifting to notes, Evernote uses "projects" and a tag hierarchy as constructs for organizing notes whereas MS OneNote organizes notes into "Section Tabs" and "Pages." In general, grouping items and the support for organization are very application-specific.

3. **Value-added data**. #2 is just a special case of a more general circumstance. Applications (or the people vending these applications) need to find ways of being better than their competition. The competitive advantage of one application over another frequently translates into metadata to be persisted for our information. To take a trivial example, an application may decide to give users an option to associate a color or an icon with each task. This is additional data that must be persisted per task (or reference or note).

As users of PIM tools, we face a more basic challenge. We have an encounter with "something"—a thought, a beautiful sunset, a Web page, the PDF of an article or a piece of music we happen to hear at a coffee shop. We wish to "capture" for use later on.

But what is "it?" And what is captured? Maybe we type a few words, take a picture, or make an audio recording (of the music or our spoken words). Or maybe we do all three. Is it a "note?" If our encounter is with an academic article, then we want to link to the article and perhaps we also try to gather reference information so that we can both read and also cite the article later on. Is it then a reference? But then perhaps we want to set a date by which we wish to do something in relation to the encounter—send the picture to our parents or recognize the music using Shazam[251] or read the article. Is "it" now a task or a to-do?

Call it a *notion.* The word has a good family history.

From **notionem** *(nom. notio) "concept," from notus, pp. of noscere "come to know" (see know)*[252].

A notion is a fragment of metadata—data about data. A notion is a bundling of attributes (with values). A notion, as metadata, can be "about" an existing information item (or even a physical thing) which is already addressed by one or more URIs. But a notion might also be about a thought, an idea, or an intention for which there is nothing to "point to" other than the notion itself.

In the Keeping Found Things Found effort, we have been able to use XML as a means to represent a notion. We have developed a schema, called *XooML*[253] to define the basic attributes and structure of a notion[254].

XooML and its uses is described in greater detail elsewhere[255]. Here we consider how the *notion* as described by XooML has the flexibility—the plasticity—we need to serve as a modular unit in the construction of our digital houses of information.

1. **The basic notion is simple.** The basic notion has only a few required attributes (including, schemaLocation to point to the schema definition for XooML and schemaVerison to specify the version of this schema in effect for the notion's XML description). The notion has a few additional, optional attributes (such as a *displayName* and a *relatedItem* for which the notion is metadata). The basic notion has no internal structure.

2. **A notion can "differentiate"** to represent a task, note, reference, calendar event or information in some other form. This is done through the inclusion, within the notion, of additional bundles of attributes—each of which is required to have an assigned namespace (i.e., a URI assignment for the xmlns attribute).

3. **A notion can differentiate to represent a grouping item**, such as a folder or tag. This is done

through an optional inclusion of outgoing (one way) links—*associations*. Associations are sub-elements in a notion. Each link has a required *ID* (a GUID[256]) and (optionally) a *displayName, associatedItem* (to specify the URI of an associated item) and *associatedXooMLFragment* (to specify the URI of a notion to use as metadata for the associated item).

4. **The links (associations) of a notion can also differentiate to represent a variety of different kinds of links.** This is done through the inclusion, within a given association of the notion, of additional bundles of attributes—each of which is required to have an assigned namespace (i.e., a URI assignment for the xmlns attribute)[257].

5. **A notion is modular.** In graph theory terms, a notion defines a node and its outgoing links. Notions in aggregate define a *multidigraph*[258].

Notions as defined by XooML are motivated by two basic needs in the construction of our digital houses of information.

1. There is a need to make structures "first class"—with tool-independent representation. Such a representation is a first step towards a digital world in which we can more freely "mix and match" tools.

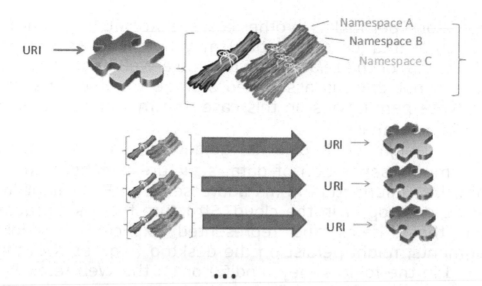

Figure 4.2: A depiction of a XooML "notion" (as a puzzle piece) with a bundle of common attributes (in brown) and additional bundles (blue, red, and green) in separate sub-elements (each of a different namespace). The notion can also have associations (dark-blue arrows) each of which also has a bundle of common attributes and additional bundles as sub-elements.

2. At the same time, a representation needs to allow for tool-specific attributes including the attributes that informally define "semi-structures" (Gestalts[259]). For example, tools may give us ways to informally group the elements of a view—by position, color, size, shape, etc. Tool-specific information is persisted in the XooML schema through a simple but effective use of namespaces to avoid attribute name collisions. This is done without the use of a "central authority."

Where do these notions, as XML fragments defined by XooML, live? Where are they stored? Several answers are possible. Planz[260] is a prototype that associates XooML fragments to file system folders in order to realize added document-like, outline-like affordances. (Folders and subfolders appear as headings and subheadings. Files appear as notes.) In this case, XooML fragments are simply kept as a files ("xooml.xml") within the folders to which they apply—one per folder. In other cases, a XooML fragment (as the representation of a notion) may not have an external *relatedItem* or the *relatedItem* may be a Web page for which there is not obvious associated storage to which the user has write permissions. In this case, the metadata might be kept in a database[261].

The design of XooML is guided by a now classic hypermedia separation of data, structure and behavior[262]. Data, i.e., information items addressed by URIs, might live on the desktop or in the cloud. Structure too, as extracted from these items and represented explicitly in XooML fragments, might persist on the desktop (e.g., as XML files stored in the folders they modify) or on the Web (e.g., in a service like S3[263] or in storage structured through a tool like SQLite[264]). XooML supports a diversity of behaviors for the same structure through a provision for tool-specific attributes—persisted both at the level of a fragment and each of its associations. This schema enables a grand vision of multiple tools all supporting a single unifying structure.

The XooML approach to notions is extremely lightweight and flexible. As noted elsewhere[265] tools might (but are not required to) use common utilities for synchronization (with the "base reality" of the relatedItem). Tools might also use in common a utility for reading and making changes to the XooML fragments that define notions. But this is all optional.

A tool might choose to create more than one sub-element per notion or per association within a notion in order to bundle different attributes under different namespaces.

Conversely, a group of tools might choose to work in a common namespace and with sub-element bundles of attributes so identified. For example, tools might work with a sub-element that bundles together the reference attributes of Dublin Core (e.g., "title," "creator," "publisher," etc.) and is identified by a Dublin Core namespace (e.g., with xmlns = http://dublincore.org/documents/dcminamespace/). The notion then differentiates to be a reference. Or tools might choose to work with sub-elements that bundle attributes for iCalendar to-dos or events.

4.1.5 OUR HOUSES ON WHEELS

This chapter has invoked the metaphor of house-building to characterize one approach to PIM in a Web-wide world of abundance in tools and storage. We look for approaches to tool integration and information representation that keep our information houses—structure and content—intact even as we make mix & match the use of various tools. This situation is depicted in Figure 4.4 as a factoring of the tool-enabled surfaces through which we view and work with our information.

Figure 4.4 further depicts a factoring of information from storage. Our information needs to be stored somewhere. Better is if it is stored in several places. And even better if we can easily pick, choose and change between storage providers as our assessment of their relative merits (for cost, reliability, speed of access, etc.) changes. Our houses on wheels. The house may move but it should stay intact.

Figure 4.3: Our information can stay whole even as it moves from one store to the next[266].

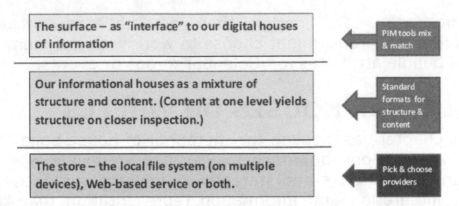

Figure 4.4: In a future, we work on/in our houses of information using any number of tools. Our houses of information may be distributed across different stores through different services.

4.2 LIVING WITH, THROUGH AND ON THE WEB

The Web is here to stay. If nothing else, people need to learn to live *with* the Web—even the small percentage of us who choose not to use the Web. At the other extreme are people who spend significant portions of their time living *on* the Web through social networking services such as Facebook or through virtual worlds such as that of Second Life. The rest of us are in a pragmatic middle. We neither avoid the Web nor do we spend much time on the Web as entertainment in its own right. The Web is a means to an end. We go to the Web for the weather forecast for today or to reserve a table at a restaurant for tomorrow's celebration. But as we make pragmatic uses of the Web (as a way to learn about and effect change in our world), our experiences of the world are mediated by the Web. We are living *through* the Web. And, whether we wish to or not, we are living on the Web.

4.2.1 LIVING *WITH* THE WEB

Do we have to have any relationship with the Web? How about living "off " or without the Web altogether? But these days, that means also giving up most of the applications we use on our computing devices. We'll slog through phone trees for information others can retrieve from the Web in a fraction of the time. We'll cling to an ever shrinking supply of newspapers and periodicals still published in paper form. Even so, we may need to check the Web from time to time to find out how the Web, so to speak, is "using" us. We might "Google" ourselves. Do we appear in pictures posted by others? Are people blogging about us? Are we the victims of "cyberspite"[267]?

4.2.2 LIVING *THROUGH* THE WEB

Many of us adopt a pragmatic approach. The Web is a very useful means to the various ends of our lives. Hotel reservations, plane tickets, gifts delivered to friends and family—we get things done through the Web. Weather reports, news articles, sports scores, stock market updates, Wikipedia articles—we're informed quickly and easily through the Web.

The Web offers us many roads easily traveled to a wider world. But, as we travel these roads, there are other roads we're not taking. We're less likely to travel to a physical library or the reference shelf at home for an encyclopedia article. As we place orders for books, electronics and even groceries on-line, we're no longer traveling older paths to brick & mortar stores. We're not experiencing incidental human contacts along the way. We're not likely to meet a friend or neighbor while shopping at Amazon.

Some might say that the Web is to information what a restaurant chain like McDonald's is to food—is served up quickly, "cheaply" (no cost, little effort) for instant gratification from the "drive-by" windows we access through our devices. The first bytes taste good. But are there hidden prices to pay later on? Is the information we receive of good quality or is it "tainted" with one-sided reportage and self-perpetuating falsehoods? Are we getting a balanced diet of information that adequately reflects different perspectives and adequately represents the complexities of the question at hand? Or are we getting fat (and "fatheaded") with sound bite information that oversimplifies and is amplified in a back and forth exchange between people who already share our views?

Authors have captured headline attention (and book sales) with provocative theses: a generation growing up with ("on") the Web will be the dumbest so far[268]. We're all becoming "stupid" through use of the Web (and web-based services like Google) or, in any case, more forgetful[269].

A counter thesis is that we are, individually and collectively, becoming much smarter through the ready availability of information on the Web. If the Web serves up an informational equivalent of junk food, it also provides rapid access to high-quality information of a kind once only found in "brick and mortar" libraries.

We can also note that seemingly with each new informational technology come a remarkably consistent litany of concerns: that in our embrace of the technology, we will become lazier, dumber, more forgetful or more susceptible to misinformation. Consider the following:

We have reason to fear that the multitude of books which grows every day in a prodigious fashion will make the following centuries fall into a state as barbarous as that of the centuries that followed the fall of the Roman Empire. Unless we try to prevent this danger by separating those books which we must throw out or leave in oblivion from those which one should save and within the latter between what is useful and that is not.

This was said by one Adrien Baillet in 1685[270].

In the Phaedrus dialog, Plato (representing Socrates) recounts a legend that questions the technology of writing itself. In the dialog, the Egyptian god Theuth speaking to King Thamus extols the virtues of writing as an enhancement of human memory. But a skeptical Thamus counters that the real effect is likely to be the opposite and that writing can only remind; it cannot help us to truly remember and may only give us the illusion of knowledge[271].

Whether the technology is our palmtop devices, the Web, or even writing itself—each new technology presents challenges as well as opportunities. The Web gives us fast, easy access to far more information than we can consume. Our challenge is to be sure the information we get is of high quality and is balanced in its portrayal of the world it means to represent. We need to question and cross-check. Wikipedia is a marvelous resource but we should consider it a point of departure for a larger exploration of the topic at hand rather than the final destination[272].

Another challenge is not to be too quickly taken by screaming headlines whether these come through the Web or more conventional, print media. The previous chapter called into question the notion that our brains (or the brains of our children) are being re-wired to support multi-tasking. But consider this screaming headline: "Study Shows Internet Alters Memory."[273] The article proceeds to say that "Researchers ... say Google and its search-engine brethren have started to reshape your brain." Moving beyond the attention-grapping lead-in, the article then provides a more balanced depiction of a scholarly article by the researchers themselves. Researchers, in their scholarly article[274], are far less sensational. People are shown less likely to commit to memory information that is readily available on the Web. They are, on the other hand, more likely to remember how to return to this information on the Web. Consciously committing information to memory is effortful. We generally don't bother for information that's readily available—whether through a paper cheatsheet, an address book or the Web. We are rational[275] in our use of our resources and our (physical) memory is one such resource. Yes, the Web is "reshaping" our brains. But so is life and living in general. We might just as well write an article that announces "Study Shows that Daily Experience Alters Memory." We should hope so.

There are many of us who live *through* the Web, i.e., we mean to make pragmatic use of the Web as a way to understand our world and as a way to get things done in our lives. For the many of us in this category, there is one more caveat: as we seek information on the Web, we are seeing only the tiniest percentage of the relevant information. People greatly overestimate the percentage of relevant information returned by a query. This finding precedes the Web and its search services[276].

In our Web-based searches, we are highly unlikely to look at information unless it appears on the first page of the results listing returned by our search engine of choice. Indeed, there is a strong bias to click the very first item in the results listing[277]. For any of several reasons, a great deal of the Web's information will not be illuminated by the "lamppost" of a particular search service[278]. We are in special need of greater tool support for exploratory searches of a kind we undertake when we are unsure what we're looking for and unsure even of the topic area[279].

Pending the availability of better tools, here are some steps we can take using existing tools and services as we try to live through the Web.

1. **Keep searching**. Pre-phrase the query. "Berry pick,"[280] i.e., use the results of one search to formulate a new query providing a slightly different angle into the pool of relevant information. Use the "Open link in new tab"

feature (now widely supported in web browsers) to open a sequence of search results in successive tabs of a browsing window.

2. **Try different search services**. If Google, Bing and Yahoo return nearly the same results, then try "alternate" search services like Blekko[281] or try one of the meta-search services[282].

3. **Try various forms of "social searching."** Mechanisms of collaborative filtering can make use of your social graph or of "people like you" to suggest other results[283]. But old-fashioned "word of mouth" and "ask a friend" can work too. Special-topic, Web-based discussion boards can also be a source of useful information.

The power provided by a new technology is never shared equally. New technologies effect a redistribution of power. But in this redistribution there are winners and losers. With the invention writing, came a special—often priestly—class of people who could write. When printing presses were new and expensive, the few who owned a printing press had a special power. Now in a Web-widened world the publishing barriers are low—we "publish" easily through personal web sites, posts to blogs and wikis, facebook, and continuously, through tweets. But now the power is with search providers. The power of Web-wide search is held in only a few hands representing a concentration of power much greater than that for printing press owners back in the late middle ages.

Looking into the future, there are, very much in the spirit of Internet, efforts to "democratize" search through distributed, peer-to-pear search services[284].

4.2.3 LIVING *ON* THE WEB

Even as we learn to live *with* the Web for the good and the bad and *through* the Web to get things done, we can't help but live *on* the Web. In extreme cases, we live virtual lives on the Web through services like Second Life[285]. But living on the Web needn't be anything as dramatic as flying through a virtual world in cartoonish bodies depicting people younger, slimmer, more stylish and just plain better looking than ourselves in physical reality.

We, or rather our informational selves, live on the Web through the traces we leave behind with nearly every interaction. We live on the Web with every account we create—Facebook, LinkedIn, Amazon, Google, Good Reads. The list goes on and on. Do we even try to keep track anymore? (Think of all our different user names and passwords!) We live on the Web with each email we send and with each picture, Tweet or status update we post. Indeed, especially if "cookies"[286] are enabled, we live on the Web with each search we make and with each web site we visit.

Information about us can be pieced together. An identity for us can be pieced together—even without our involvement or consent. We can take steps to protect our identity—traveling "incognito"[287], for example, or through proxy server[288]. But for these services, we lose some of the benefits of "being known"—the benefits of cookies, for example, to personalize our interactions with participating web sites.

Anonymity on the Web may not be possible and may not be desirable either. Instead, we might accept the inevitability of a Web presence and then take active steps to manage this presence. If we choose to do so, here are some developments to consider:

OpenID as a way to consolidate our many different logins and passwords[289]. Related to OpenID is the notion of a personal URI[290].

"OnLine Presence," as the outer appearance of your information house[291] and as managed in any number of ways. You may create a "personal wiki," for example[292], or a portfolio Web site[293].

4.2.4 THE OBJECTS OF OUR APPLICATIONS, PART II: BUILDING OUR STORIES

"Object" and "application" allow for several distinct meanings. In the previous section, we considered objects such as tasks, notes and references as digital things to be linked to and structured through our software applications. In this concluding portion of the current section, consider, instead, "object" as a goal or purpose and "application" as in the application of our resources—our expertise, energy, attention and, especially, our time. What now is the object of our application? What are we trying to realize?

From this perspective, references, notes and tasks are not "the objects of our applications." References are part of a larger effort with the object to complete an article for publication or a term paper for a good grade. Notes are so we won't forget or so we can be informed. Tasks are part of a larger effort—which we often call a project. The object might be to "have a fun family vacation someplace warm that doesn't cost too much" or the object might be to "get a job" or "get a promotion" or "get a good performance review."

Moreover, some of the larger objects we've discussed in the previous section—documents, presentations and spreadsheets, for example—aren't the objects of our applications either. A document or a presentation may be to inform, impress or incite to action. If so, a one-on-one conversation during a golf game might do just as well. Or perhaps a blog post plus follow-on commentary (providing the right people are participating) or even a sequence of Tweets.

Let's consider the story as an object in both senses of the word. A good, well-constructed story is both the thing we work on (as supported through a mix-and-match of tools) and also the point of our efforts—to be told repeatedly and to be used in many different ways[294].

We consider first the story as the thing told in relation to any project—any endeavor—that we undertake whether for play or work. The story of an endeavor is told first in future tense as an intention (what do we want to do?), then in an extended present tense as execution (what are we, should we be doing now?) and finally (and repeatedly) in the past tense as reflections and reminiscences (what did we do?).

Second, we consider the stories we tell as we try to understand something new like a term paper topic or something old like a family history or a life-long research interest. These are open-ended stories often told in no particular order or in many different orders (as we seek to understand). These are often stories with no ending.

Stories told in future, present and past tense

We have a notion—something we want to make happen, to realize. Perhaps it's something work-related—a re-organization is being imposed from above with lots of moving pieces and lots of unknowns. We want to be sure it works out best for us and the people in our group. Or perhaps it's a trip we've long talked about doing with our family. Or a home re-model.

Every project—every endeavor—is told as a story. The story is told in different tenses. First, in the future tense. What do we want to accomplish? What will things look like when we're done? What are the constraints? What do we need to be sure *not* to do? Later, the story is told in an extended present tense as we attempt to make good on our plans. What next? Our inner voice may be providing narrative with comments like "Hurry up or we'll be late!" Finally, the story is told, often repeatedly, in the past tense. Snippets are told at dinner parties or as casual elevator conversation or as Facebook posts. The story may be told more formally, more completely in a final or "post mortem" report.

We need distinctly different tools for each stage of the project—each tense of the story. Consider the story of a home remodel.

1. **Future tense**. Planning of the house re-model may involve an initial brainstorm: Which rooms to change? How? Whom to use as an architect? Whom to use as the contractor? What's the budget? When should the re-model be done? At this stage we might use a mind-mapping tool such as FreeMind[295]. Or possibly we use OneNote or Evernote as a way to capture a lot of ideas along with links to the information items (email messages, Web pages) that inspired these. If we have too many notions at one level (e.g., ideas or snippets of information) we may look for a tool to compose or "chunk" elemental notions into higher-level notions (e.g., "kitchen countertops" or "architects we might use"). We may post portions of our plan to a blog so that others know what we're up to and can offer advice and pointers to relevant information.

2. **Present tense**. Our needs shift dramatically as we move to the execution stage of the project. Our focus shifts to matters of schedule, scope and the availability of resources (money, time and the expertise of others). Even so, the structure—e.g., the mind map—generated in the planning phase is a reasonable starting point for this stage as interpreted by more workflow-oriented

tools such as Microsoft Project or OmniFocus or the outline view provided by the Planz prototype[296].

3. **Past tense**. Finally, in the review stage, we tell stories about what happened. The story may be told formally as a complete report but, more often, it is told in snippets: The things that went especially well or especially poorly, the subcontractor who smoked in the house, the funny incident with the raccoon, the clever solution for a closet in the guest bedroom ... Again the tool selection changes. Again, we may post to a blog. Or we may post pictures to our Facebook or Flickr account. Using a tool such as MS Word we may even decide to create our own "My re-model" magazine to be distributed in printed and electronic form.

Even as each stage calls for its own set of tools, the activities and associated information of the stages might be unified, in different overlays, by a shared structure: many tools; one structure. During initial planning, the primary structure may be location-based according to the rooms in the house that we hope to re-model. During execution of the plan, the structure may also include a temporal overlay to mark off phases of the project and the regions of the house impacted by each phase (especially important if we plan to continue living in the house during the re-model). In a retrospective, we may add structure to mark off re-modeling vignettes that might be especially interesting or funny to tell to other people.

Why story-telling? For one thing, stories told in the future tense as expressions of intention—especially if these contain specifics concerning the "how" of execution—are more likely to come true than if we merely expressed a vaguely worded desire to "finish the re-model"[297]. As our story develops into a plan, we're more likely to experience moments of serendipity where relevant information or the right person just "happens" to appear[298].

For another thing, we love to "tell a good yarn"[299]. We tell stories all the time and enjoy doing so. When asked to tag something—an article, a picture, a video—people may take time and struggle. They are not sure what tags they should use. But people readily tell stories for the same objects. And from the words of these stories come tags that are often of better quantity and quality than those generated during an explicit exercise to "tag"[300].

Stories, as indexed for fast search, can be an excellent way to organize related materials—photographs, drawings, email exchanges, etc. And these days, the recipients of our digital stories can talk back—encouraging us to clarify or elaborate on this or that point.

Consider the story of Jill and her summer vacation in Italy. She took lots of pictures. But the pictures in Jill's camera, or later on her hard drive, were a source of guilt and foreboding ("I really should do something with these pictures before I forget ... "What if I lose them or delete them???!!"). Fortunately, Jill decided to post many of these photos on the Web (e.g., to a site such as Facebook or Flickr). She wrote captions. The sequence of pictures and their captions tell a story of her summer vacation. Her travel companions comment. Other friends comment. Jill comments on these comments. As this happens the story is told in greater detail. In this way, storytelling is a social interaction that happens over time and, potentially, across great distances. The story is fun to tell at the time. It's hardly work at all. But some 20 or 30 years later the story may be an invaluable part of Jill's "house of information"— helping her to remember and reminisce over what might otherwise be "just a bunch of old pictures."

A never-ending story[301]

Those of us involved in academic research know that papers, articles and presentations are rarely built from scratch. These are constructed, instead, from our previous papers, articles and presentations. Something similar happened when I was called upon to write a semi-annual report in my non-academic places of work or, long ago, when I would begin to write a new function in LISP. I would almost always look for a "given" in order to build the "new." Even when the given differed greatly from the intended new in content, I could still use its structure as a template.

But often content as well as structure is borrowed from our previous work. This is not done as a shameless act of "self-plagiarism" but rather in a practical program of re-use. A paragraph of clear, concise explanation or a compelling graphic deserves to be re-used—sometimes in a written report, certainly as a slide (or talking point) in an oral presentation.

The ability to communicate clearly—to inform—is important in many walks of life—not just in academia. Over the years, our expertise grows and we may have the sense that we are telling variations of the same story over and over again. Our stories are updated with new information or as our knowledge for an area grows, but much in the stories we tell today is recognizably similar to that we told in stories years ago.

Re-use of the good stuff ought to be easier. Can we remember times when we looked in vain for something we'd done previously? Or came upon it only after the opportunity for re-use had passed? At the same time, a tired re-use of the "same old, same old" ought to be easier to detect.

Suppose all of our writings, all of our drawings, all of our good thoughts as expressed were represented in an interconnected network of paragraph- or "slide"-sized notions? If the network is an expression of our professional expertise then, in keeping with the "houses of information" metaphor, this network might form our "home office."

The notion that small chunks of information might be richly interconnected to define a network of re-useable information is not new. A similar vision motivated the Zog effort of the 1970s[302]. The vision has been expressed through prototypes like NoteCards[303], and also through commercial products like HyperCard[304] or, more recently, DevonThink[305].

But creating, maintaining and making effective use of such a network is not easy. There is certainly more to do than can be supported by a single tool. Our inter-connected notions and the structure they define should be "first class"—with existence outside and separate from any given tool but accessible and able to be worked on by many different tools. The document or the presentation is then no longer the "object." The network is the object. We pick and choose—we group together—notions of the network as needed to create this document or that presentation. We might then have one tool able to detect when the truly "new" in a new document or presentation has fallen below a certain percentage as determined by settings we provide. After all, we don't want to get "stale."

And now consider another example—a team term paper done by a group of students (usually 3 or 4) to satisfy a major requirement for a college course. A student once told me that the actual paper his team produced was only the "tip of the iceberg." Beneath the surface were many, many email exchanges, blog posts, a draft-paper use of Google Docs and even some tweets via Twitter. These many forms of information were all a part of an extended dialog that proved very helpful to the students in their effort to complete the project. But, the student lamented, what a shame that this activity below the surface couldn't be surfaced for greater visibility and re-use!

Could it be that someday this dialog, this network of notion-sized interactions, could even become the primary thing to be delivered? That's hard to imagine. The dialog that was so simulating for team members might be gibberish to the professor or even to the students themselves later on.

Even so, a tantalizing notion lingers that we might be able to realize a perfect combination of orality and literacy[306]—of informal dialog and formal dissertation—an original dream of hypertext[307] realized at last.

In Plato's Phaedrus dialog, Socrates is quoted as saying: "Furthermore, writings are silent; they cannot speak, answer questions, or come to their own defense." But our stories as told on the Web through the "voices" of many different people could be very vocal indeed. Our stories told on the Web might be told as a group effort in support an ongoing never-ending dialog—stories told repeatedly but each time a little better and with a little more understanding.

4.3 CONCLUSION

Forever on the Web ... Information as a crystalline solid rather than a flowing liquid ... An information house that we build and extend, that we live with and "in"...

When we begin to think in these terms, it is no longer acceptable that a switch from one tool to the next should require an export and then an import. The process is too time-consuming and too likely to result in error. We can't convert all our information and the portion converted loses, at minimum, its original context. We look, instead, for tools that can make "house calls"—tools that can work with our information in its place.

As our applications, our ways of doing things and as we increasingly work through the Web, we should *expect* a revolution in the way our tools work. Look for tools that work *horizontally* in ways that cross and integrate the various forms of information (documents, spreadsheets, presentations, tasks, references, etc.) that have been established by traditional vertically integrated applications such as MS Word or by web-based "everything buckets" such as Evernote. Look for tools that work to support a specific kind of PIM activity (and a stage in the information life cycle) such as keeping and capture or reminding and refinding.

We have to be realistic. The transition from a reliance on vertically integrated to horizontally integrated tools will happen gradually, piecemeal and opportunistically. New tools will chip away at the monoliths, taking this function or that for horizontal integration. Big documents may increasingly become an afterthought—generated, as needed, from a network of small, modular "notions" in order to satisfy an older requirement (or the needs of a more traditional person).

As our tools work through the Web, we work through the Web. As our tools increasingly work *on the Web*, we work and live on the Web. Our Web-based information—our digital houses of information—are a reflection of and a proxy for us. We need to keep up appearances. We should be sure, metaphorically speaking, that the house's address is visible from the street, the lawn is mowed and the external walls painted from time to time. We want our walls to have function as well as form. Our walls should keep out those who would snoop, steal or vandalize. At the same time we need roads to connect our information houses to a vastly larger, web-widened world of information. It is down these roads that we send and receive information to realize our life roles and goals.

---

[162] http://en.wikipedia.org/wiki/TCP/IP_model.

[163] http://en.wikipedia.org/wiki/Internet.

[164] http://en.wikipedia.org/wiki/URI. See also, http://en.wikipedia.org/wiki/XRI.

[165] Anderson and Wolff (2010) argued for the demise of the Web in favor of the Internet; but see also Hansen, E. (2010).

[166] Jones, W. (2010) referred to information as "data in motion" as a counterpoint to the description of knowledge as "information in action" Zins, C. (2007). We might then say that wisdom is "knowledge in perspective."

[167] See "The Beginner's Guide to SEO" (http://www.seomoz.org/beginners-guide-to-seo). See also (http://www.seomoz.org/beginners-guide-to-seo, http://www.celtnet.org.uk/info/long_tail.php, http://en.wikipedia.org/wiki/SEO).

[168] http://en.wikipedia.org/wiki/Semantic_Web, http://www.scientificamerican.com/article.cfm?id=the-semantic-web, http://www.w3.org/2001/sw/.

[169] See Volz et al. (2009) and also http://en.wikipedia.org/wiki/Linked_data.

[170] See http://webtrends.about.com/od/revi3/fr/kinset_rev.htm.

[171] http://en.wikipedia.org/wiki/Metaverse.

[172] http://www.noupe.com/design/the-future-of-the-web-where-will-we-be-in-five-years.html.

[173] http://en.wikipedia.org/wiki/Yogi_Berra.

[174] http://catcode.com/teachmod.

[175] The original 3 R's stood for reading, 'riting, and 'rithmetic (http://en.wikipedia.org/wiki/The_three_Rs; see also Papert, S. (1993).

[176] http://en.wiktionary.org/wiki/execute.

[177] We can, for example, choose from crowd-sourcing options for contract work such as Amazon Mechanical Turk (MTurk) (https://www.mturk.com/mturk/welcome, see also http://en.wikipedia.org/wiki/Amazon_Mechanical_Turk).

[178] http://en.wikipedia.org/wiki/3D_printing.

[179] The potential combined uses of the Web and a palmtop are staggering. Find just the right restaurant nearby as we walk through the streets of Paris. Find friends too. Track our path as an overlay to a map of Paris. Send out path to a friend or loved one and they too can have some of our experience. Through a full-motion video camera we wear? Maybe. But the availability of the Web allows for other options. Send only the path, possibly as enhanced by a few pictures we take, and let our friends and family experience a "street view" of the path in Google Earth.

[180] Services that come to us are to be contrasted with existing services (e.g., priceline.com) where we can "go" to bid for goods and services.

[181] http://theappslab.com/2009/09/03/what-software-do-you-most-often/.

[182]See, for example,
http://www.dailytech.com/Office+2010+to+Launch+Today+Microsoft+Owns+94+Percent+of+the+Market/article18360.htm.

[183]http://al3x.net/2009/01/31/against-everything-buckets.html,
http://lifehacker.com/5666954/avoid-everything-buckets-aka-why-i-cant-get-into-apps-like-evernote.

[184]We explore a different sense of "object" in the next section ("Living with, through and on the Web") in a sub-section titled "The objects of our application, Part II: Building our stories."

[185]http://en.wikipedia.org/wiki/List_of_office_suites;
http://en.wikipedia.org/wiki/Comparison_of_office_suites.

[186]http://en.wikipedia.org/wiki/Microsoft_Office; http://office.microsoft.com/en-us.

[187]http://en.wikipedia.org/wiki/OpenOffice.org; http://www.openoffice.org/.

[188]http://en.wikipedia.org/wiki/Software_as_a_service (see also, Turner et al. (2003)).

[189]http://www.bizcommunity.com/Article/224/23/59579.html.

[190]http://www.microsoft.com/en-us/office365/free-office365-trial.aspx?WT.srch=1&WT.mc_id=PS_google_Office+365_Entice_office%20365_Text#fbid=tvgcxxuur1B; For a review of Office 365, see,
http://www.pcmag.com/article2/0,2817,2383731,00.asp. For a comparison with Google Apps see: http://www.infoworld.com/d/cloud-computing/office-365-vs-google-apps-the-infoworld-review-447.

[191]http://www.pcmag.com/article2/0,2817,2365016,00.asp.

[192]http://en.wikipedia.org/wiki/Rich_Internet_application.

[193]Calore, M. (2010), Rist, O. (2006).

[194]http://en.wikipedia.org/wiki/HTML5, http://www.w3.org/TR/html5/.

[195]Weinreich et al. (2008).

[196]Adar et al. (2009).

[197]Weinreich et al. (2008).

[198]For example, an unpublished 1998 study was conducted (by Kirsten Ridden) to assess user experiment with of "Search Clips" (United States Patent #6,256,623, http://patft.uspto.gov/netacgi/nph-Parser?Sect1=PTO2&Sect2=HITOFF&u=/netahtml/PTO/search-adv.htm&r=109&p=3&f=G&l=50&d=PTXT&S1=6256623&OS=+6256623&RS=6256623). We see search clips now in both Bing and Google. For example, in results returned by Bing in response to a query sent on January 27, 2012 for "flights to Maui from Seattle" I received the following:

Flights from **Seattle, WA** to **Maui, HI**

FROM	TO	WEEKEND ESTIMATES
Seattle, WA (SEA) - Seat	Kahului, HI (OGG) - Kahul	$582 Depart February 03

LEAVE	RETURN	
02/17/2012	02/19/2012	Find flights

$661 Depart February 10

$935 Depart February 17

bing.com/travel

In the study, participants experienced (for different queries) each of two conditions: 1. Control: Click on a traditional result to see a new provider Web page that included a content-specific fielded search clip (such as that shown above). 2. Search clip variation: Click to see the same search clip displayed in the context of the search service UI. In both conditions, a new Web page was presented with the same speed (both pages were actually local files on the participant's experimental machine). However, less changed visually in condition #2 and participants experienced this condition as being faster.

[199]See, for example, http://www.web3mantra.com/2011/04/20/best-html5-applications/.

[200]http://en.wikipedia.org/wiki/Visual_Basic_for_Applications.

[201]http://www.straightdope.com/columns/read/1575/whats-the-origin-of-the-expression-from-soup-to-nuts.

[202]Vertical integration is often used in a corporate context to describe an aggregation of services and products in a supply chain under a common owner. An example is a large oil company that owns all aspects of petroleum production from the drilling platform to the pump. (See, http://en.wikipedia.org/wiki/Vertical_integration, and also, http://www.economist.com/node/13396061.)

[203]With respect to Facebook we have the reassuring words from Mark Zuckerberg that people "People Own and Control Their Information" (http://blog.facebook.com/blog.php?post=54434097130) but countering viewpoints proliferate (see, for example, http://www.npr.org/templates/story/story.php?storyId=100783689, http://mashable.com/2009/02/16/facebook-tos-privacy/, http://consumerist.com/2009/02/facebooks-new-terms-of-service-we-can-do-anything-we-want-with-your-content-forever.html or search for "who owns our information on Face-book?").

[204]Consider, for example, the Sidekick fiasco (http://en.wikipedia.org/wiki/2009_Sidekick_data_loss; http://www.pcworld.com/article/173470/microsoft_redfaced_after_massive_sidekick_data_loss.html, or search for "sidekick data loss").

[205]GeoCities, for example, shutdown (http://news.slashdot.org/story/09/10/26/1359223/geocities-shutting-down-today, http://mashable.com/2009/04/23/geocities-shutdown/). Or consider the uncertain fate of the Delicious tagging service

(http://www.geekosystem.com/yahoo-shutting-down-delicious/;
http://www.pcmag.com/article2/0,2817,2374446,00.asp;
http://www.huffingtonpost.com/2010/12/16/delicious-shutting-down-y_n_797927.html#s210069&title=Ross_).

[206] With apologies to Arthur C. Clarke whose monoliths were large, multi-function machines (built by some unseen extraterrestrial) that appeared in his Space Odyssey series (see
http://en.wikipedia.org/wiki/Monolith_(Space_Odyssey).

[207] For discussions on feature use, see http://www.quora.com/Microsoft-Word/Do-people-know-how-to-use-Microsoft-Office; http://googlesystem.blogspot.com/2008/02/most-frequently-used-features-in.html; http://www.pluggd.in/microsoft/most-used-features-commands-in-microsoft-word-and-a-few-design-lessons-2600/ or search for "how many features in MS Word are used by the average user?"

[208] The Swiss Army Knife picture does in fact exist and can be purchased (http://www.amazon.com/Wenger-16999-Giant-Swiss-Knife/dp/B001DZTJRQ).

[209] For MS Word for example, http://www.faughnan.com/msword.html or http://www.facebook.com/groups/2209479541/. For Facebook, try http://www.i-marco.nl/weblog/archive/2009/04/14/five_reasons_why_i_hate_facebook or http://www.joecrazy.com/10-reasons-hate-facebook/. Alternatively, search with the pattern "<monolith name> sucks" as in http://www.shamusyoung.com/twentysidedtale/?p=11809. Of course the Web will yield results even when "hate" is replaced with "love"—only opinions do not seem to be stated with quite as much passion.

[210] Horizontal integration in a corporate context refers to a strategy in which a company seeks to sell a type of product in numerous markets (see http://en.wikipedia.org/wiki/Horizontal_integration). In the context of PIM, horizontal integration additionally might refer to efforts to support a kind of activity—such as capture and keeping or reminding and re-finding —across many different forms of information.

[211] For Mendeley, Zotero and Endnote, respectively, see http://www.mendeley.com/, http://www.zotero.org/, http://www.endnote.com/. Endnote now supports extensions to take advantage of the Web (see https://www.myendnoteweb.com/EndNoteWeb.html).

[212] http://www.evernote.com/; http://office.microsoft.com/en-us/onenote/.

[213] http://www.rememberthemilk.com; http://www.omnigroup.com/products/omnifocus/; http://office.microsoft.com/en-us/outlook-help/create-tasks-and-to-do-items-HA001229302.aspx.

[214] For a comparison of reference managers see: http://en.wikipedia.org/wiki/Comparison_of_reference_management_software.

[215] http://feedback.mendeley.com/forums/4941-mendeley-feedback/suggestions/372255-zotero-2-way-sync; see also:

http://forums.zotero.org/discussion/6174/mendeley/.

[216] http://dublincore.org/, (see also, http://www.loc.gov/marc/, http://www.loc.gov/marc/bibliographic/ecbdhome.html).

[217] http://en.wikipedia.org/wiki/Citation_Style_Language, http://www.zotero.org/styles; http://citationstyles.org/.

[218] http://en.wikipedia.org/wiki/SQLite. Both Zotero and Mendeley use SQLite.

[219] http://feedback.mendeley.com/forums/4941-mendeley-feedback? filter=top&page=3.

[220] For reviews of note managers, see: http://iphone.appstorm.net/roundups/productivity-roundups/13-notable-note-taking-apps-for-iphone/; http://lifehacker.com/399556/five-best-note+taking-tools; http://mashable.com/2008/08/19/online-note-taking-applications/; http://iphone.appstorm.net/roundups/productivity-roundups/13-notable-note-taking-apps-for-iphone/; http://web.appstorm.net/roundups/data-management-roundups/the-24-best-apps-to-remember-everything-you-discover-online/ or simply search on "note-taking."

[221] http://lifehacker.com/5666954/avoid-everything-buckets-aka-why-i-cant-get-into-apps-like-evernote.

[222] http://www.priacta.com/Articles/Comparison_of_GTD_Software.php.

[223] See for example, http://web.appstorm.net/roundups/task-management/task-management-on-the-web-in-2010/; http://www.cyberciti.biz/tips/open-source-project-management-software.html.

[224] For "reviews of OmniFocus" see http://shawnblanc.net/2010/10/omnifocus/, http://www.techrepublic.com/blog/mac/review-omnifocus-for-mac/885.

[225] http://www.danielmclark.com/gtd-omnifocus-vs-remember-the-milk-on-mac-and-iphone.html; http://www.nydiscovery.com/massivemileage/2009/9/13/remember-the-milk-vs-omnifocus-task-management.html; http://jameswharris.wordpress.com/2011/03/03/outlook-tasks-v-remember-the-milk-v-toodledo/.

[226] http://shawnblanc.net/2009/01/a-review-of-two-things/.

[227] When I talk to people about their systems of task management, they seem to refer to task managers either in the future tense ("I'm going to try *name of task manager*") or the past tense ("I used to use *name of task manager* but haven't in a while ...").

[228] We notice a large overlap with the attributes of a calendar appointment or a meeting request and, in fact, iCalendar (http://en.wikipedia.org/wiki/ICalendar; http://tools.ietf.org/html/rfc5545.) often forms the basis for export and import of task information from one task manager to the next.

[229] For a study of user comparisons between "label this" (tagging) and "put that there" (foldering) models, see Civan et al. (2008).

[230] One of the earlier cross-form desktop search facilities was "Stuff I've Seen," Dumais et al. (2003).

[231] For reviews of on-line photo editors see: http://www.convertdirect.com/online_photo_editor.html; http://www.blograzzi.net/75-free-online-image-and-photo-editing-toolswebsites.html.

[232] http://www.photoshop.com/.

[233] http://www.wired.com/gadgets/wireless/magazine/17-03/mf_netbooks?currentPage=3.

[234] http://www.wired.com/gadgets/wireless/magazine/17-03/mf_netbooks?currentPage=3.

[235] http://www.openoffice.org/.

[236] http://www.softmaker.com/english/of_en.htm.

[237] For discussions of alternatives to MS Office and the extent of their compatibility with MS Office applications see: http://office-software-review.toptenreviews.com/home-office/softmaker-office-review.html; http://www.infoworld.com/d/applications/better-office-alternative-softmaker-office-bests-openofficeorg-445?page=0,2lhttp://www.infoworld.com/d/applications/office-compatibility-torture-test-302? source=fssr, http://www.macworld.com/article/133922/2008/06/iworkoffice.html.

[238] http://www.infoworld.com/d/applications/why-microsoft-office-so-hard-kill-264.

[239] Furnas, G. (1986).

[240] http://en.wikipedia.org/wiki/Dropbox_(service)#Criticism, http://dereknewton.com/2011/04/dropbox-authentication-static-host-ids/; but see also http://lifehacker.com/5527055/the-cleverest-ways-touse-dropbox-that-youre-not-using.

[241] http://windows.microsoft.com/en-US/windows7/Share-files-with-someone.

[242] http://lifehacker.com/5064688/free-online-storage-feature+by+feature-comparison-chart; http://www.informationweek.com/news/storage/reviews/231000787; http://lifehacker.com/5064688/index.php?op=showcustomobject&postId=5064688&item=0 or search for "cloud storage."

[243] With apologies to Kessy (2006). (*Sometimes a Great Notion.* Penguin Classics) and to the unknown blues artist who first sang the lyrics: "Sometimes I lives in the country; Sometimes I lives in town; Sometimes I have a great notion; To jump into the river an' drown."

[244] Our folder structure is preserved in the switch from one tool to the next. However, switching is not completely loss or trouble-free since settings for synchronization and sharing will not generally transfer from one tool to the next.

[245] http://en.wikipedia.org/wiki/Office_Open_XML.

[246] http://dublincore.org/; http://en.wikipedia.org/wiki/Metadata_registry; http://en.wikipedia.org/wiki/Dublin_Core.

[247] http://dublincore.org/documents/dces/.

[248] http://en.wikipedia.org/wiki/Digital_photography.

[249] See http://en.wikipedia.org/wiki/ICalendar for an overview and http://tools.ietf.org/html/rfc5545 for the specification. For example, there is the notion of a to-do (VTODO) with a provision for attributes for organizer, due date/time, and status. For the XML format for iCalendar, see http://tools.ietf.org/html/rfc6321.

[250] Tasks might be stored, for example, in a simple one-file database as managed through SQLite.

[251] http://www.shazam.com/.

[252] http://www.etymonline.com/index.php?term=notion; see also, http://en.wiktionary.org/wiki/notion.

[253] XooML (pronounced "zoom'l") stands for Cross (**X**) **Too**l **M**ark-up **L**anguage. For a complete definition see kftf.ischool.washington.edu/XMLschema/0.41/XooML.xsd.

[254] XooML *fragments* can be dynamically assembled into a coherent document or document like view (as they are in the Planz prototype). We have also referred to the fragment of metadata as a *noodle* to emphasis the basic node + outgoing link structure provided for in a XooML fragment. In this chapter, the word "notion" is more evocative concerning the many uses of a XooML fragment.

[255] Jones, W. (2011); Jones and Anderson (2011).

[256] http://en.wikipedia.org/wiki/Globally_unique_identifier.

[257] For example, with the addition of a *predicate* attribute (with URI as value), an association might represent an RDF subject-predicate-object statement with the notion's relatedItem serving as the subject and the association's associatedItem serving as the object.

[258] See, for example, Bollobas, Bela; *Modern Graph Theory*, Springer; 1 st ed. (August 12, 2002). With the optional addition of attributes for the associations of a node, XooML notions in aggregate can also define a hypergraph—i.e., a graph structure in which a given link can have more than two nodes.

[259] http://en.wikipedia.org/wiki/Gestalt_psychology; http://graphicdesign.spokanefalls.edu/tutorials/process/gestaltprinciples/gestal

tprinc.htm.

[260]Jones et al. (2010).

[261]Fragments might, for example, be kept in a SQLite file to which the user has write access.

[262]Nürnberg et al. (1996).

[263]http://aws.amazon.com/s3/.

[264]http://sqlite.org/.

[265]Jones and Anderson (2011).

[266]The picture is taken from: http://www.comingunmoored.com/page/20/.

[267]See http://www.newscientist.com/article/mg19826577.000-how-to-protect-your-good-name-against-cyberspite.html; http://www.eurekalert.org/pub_releases/2008-05/ns-dlc052108.php, or search on "cyberspite" or "cyber spite." Or look for "reputation management" services like http://www.reputation.com/ or http://ironreputation.com/.

[268]Bauerlein, M. (2008). See also http://www.dumbestgeneration.com/reviews.html.

[269]Carr, N. (2008). For an opposing viewpoint ("Smarter, Happier, More Productive"), see Holt, J. (2011). See also http://en.wikipedia.org/wiki/Is_Google_Making_Us_Stupid%3F.

[270]As noted by Blair, A. (2003).

[271]The distinction between reminding and true remembrance is, remarkably, raised again more recently in the context of lifelogs and a full-motion video recording of events (Sellen and Whittaker, 2010). For a charming modern day variation of the dialog used to explore the issues raised by Carr, Holt and others see Grudin, J. (2011).

[272]For a discussion on the misuses and appropriate uses of Wikipedia, see Head and Eisenberg (2010).

[273]http://slatest.slate.com/posts/2011/07/15/google_memory_change_columbia_science_magazine_recent_study_reve.html?from=rss/&wpisrc=newsletter_slatest.

[274]Sparrow et al. (2011).

[275]Anderson, J. (1990).

[276]Blair and Maron (1985).

[277]Teevan et al. (2011).

[278]See Bergman, M. (2001) and also http://en.wikipedia.org/wiki/Invisible_Web.

[279]Marchionini, G. (2006).

[280]Bates, M. (1989).

[281]http://blekko.com/; see also, http://en.wikipedia.org/wiki/Blekko.

[282]http://www.lib.berkeley.edu/TeachingLib/Guides/Internet/MetaSearch.html; http://www.zdnet.com/news/meta-search-more-heads-better-than-one/142073.

[283]For "social search" try Chi, E. (2009) and http://en.wikipedia.org/wiki/Social_search.

[284]For "distributed search" see http://en.wikipedia.org/wiki/Distributed_search_engine; http://distributedsearch.blogspot.com/; or http://wiki.apache.org/solr/DistributedSearch. Or try one of the distributed search services such as YaCy (http://yacy.net/en/, but see also http://en.wikipedia.org/wiki/YaCy) or Faroo (http://www.faroo.com/hp/p2p/p2p.html, but see also http://en.wikipedia.org/wiki/Faroo).

[285]See Kaplan and Haenlein (2009a,b), Lillie, R. (2009).

[286]http://en.wikipedia.org/wiki/HTTP_cookie. To see what Google already "knows" about you try: www.google.com/ads/preferences.

[287]http://support.google.com/chrome/bin/answer.py?hl=en&answer=95464, but see http://www.cbronline.com/blogs/technology/how_secret_is_g.

[288]See, for example, http://www.anonymizer.com/ or http://www.hidemyass.com/.

[289]http://openid.net/. See also, http://en.wikipedia.org/wiki/OpenID.

[290]Weitzner, D. (2007).

[291]Your on-line resume (as part of your on-line presence) will certainly replace or dominate more conventional methods of "selling" yourself in the job market. See http://www.forbes.com/sites/danschawbel/2011/02/21/5-reasons-why-your-online-presence-will-replace-your-resume-in-10-years/; or http://www.zdnet.com/blog/security/ten-little-things-to-secure-your-online-presence/9901?pg=2&tag=content;siu-container.

[292]http://en.wikipedia.org/wiki/Personal_wiki; http://en.wikipedia.org/wiki/Personal_wiki.

[293]http://www.smashingmagazine.com/2009/02/26/10-steps-to-the-perfect-portfolio-website/; http://webdesign.about.com/od/jobs/a/aa102207.htm.

[294]The word "story" also has distinct meanings that fit nicely with this chapter's dominant theme of "building our houses of digital information." Story as "an account of real or fictional events" (http://en.wiktionary.org/wiki/story, noun sense #1) but also story "as a floor or level of a building; a storey" (http://en.wiktionary.org/wiki/story, noun sense #2). A story as a tale may be "so called because the fronts of buildings in the Middle Ages often were decorated with rows of painted windows" (http://www.etymonline.com/index.php?term=story).

[295] http://freemind.sourceforge.net/wiki/index.php/Main_Page.

[296] Jones et al. (2010).

[297] See research on intention by Gollwitzer and colleagues, for example: Gollwitzer and Sheeran (2006); Sheeran et al. (2005).

[298] There is generally little that is accidental about these encounters. We may be constantly encountering information that could be useful to us in our efforts to reach this or that goal. But unless thoughts of a goal and the steps we need to take towards its fulfillment, are active in our minds, we may easily overlook the information. (For a study of opportunism in information encounters see Seifert and Patalano (2001).)

[299] Hsu, J. (2008). See also a post on story-telling on KeepingFoundThingsFound.com (http://keepingfoundthingsfound.com/blog/can-stories-help-us-organize-and-make-sense-our-information).

[300] Marshall, C. (2009).

[301] With apologies to Michael Ende and his excellent book, Ende, M. (1997). *The Neverending Story.* (R. Manheim, Trans.) (First American Edition). Dutton Juvenile. (See also, http://en.wikipedia.org/wiki/The_Neverending_Story).

[302] http://en.wikipedia.org/wiki/ZOG_(hypertext).

[303] Halasz, F., 1988, Halasz et al., 1987.

[304] http://en.wikipedia.org/wiki/HyperCard.

[305] http://www.devontechnologies.com/products/devonthink/overview.html.

[306] Ong, W. (2007). See also http://en.wikipedia.org/wiki/Orality.

[307] Nelson, T. (1982).

Bibliography

Abiteboul, S., Bonifati, A., Cobéna, G., Manolescu, I., and Milo, T. (2003) Dynamic XML documents with distribution and replication. *Proceedings of the 2003 ACM SIGMOD international conference on Management of data* (pp. 527–538). San Diego, California: ACM. DOI: 10.1145/872757.872821 Cited on page(s) 36

Adamczyk, P. D., and Bailey, B. P. (2004) If not now, when?: the effects of interruption at different moments within task execution. *Proceedings of the SIGCHI conference on Human factors in computing systems* (pp. 271–278). Vienna, Austria: ACM. DOI: 10.1145/985692.985727 Cited on page(s) 49, 51

Adar, E., Teevan, J., and Dumais, S. T. (2009) Resonance on the web: web dynamics and revisitation patterns. *Proceedings of the 27th international conference on Human factors in computing systems* (pp. 1381–1390). Boston, MA, USA: ACM. DOI: 10.1145/1518701.1518909 Cited on page(s) 63

Aftab, O., Cheung, P., Kim, A., Thakkar, S., and Yeddanapudi, N. (2001) *Information theory and the digital age*. Cambridge, MA: Massachusetts Institute of Technology. Retrieved from http://web.mit.edu/6.933/www/projects_whole.html Cited on page(s) 1

Ahern, S., Eckles, D., Good, N. S., King, S., Naaman, M., and Nair, R. (2007) Over-exposed?: privacy patterns and considerations in online and mobile photo sharing.

Proceedings of the SIGCHI conference on Human factors in computing systems (pp. 357–366). San Jose, California, USA: ACM. DOI: 10.1145/1240624.1240683 Cited on page(s) 40

Allen (2008) Dredging up the past: lifelogging, memory and surveillance. *Univ. Chicago Law Rev.* 75:47–74. Cited on page(s) 40

Anderson, Chris, and Wolff, Michael. (2010), August 17). The Web Is Dead. Long Live the Internet | Magazine. *Wired Magazine*. Retrieved March 23, 2011, from http://www.wired.com/magazine/2010/08/ff_webrip/ Cited on page(s) 55

Anderson, J. R. (1990) *The adaptive character of thought*. Hillsdale, NJ: Lawrence Erlbaum Associates. Cited on page(s) 85

Anderson, P. (2007) What is Web 2.0? Ideas, technologies and implications for education. *JISC Technology and Standards Watch*. Cited on page(s) 59

Barreau, D. (2008) The persistence of behavior and form in the organization of personal information. *J. Am. Soc. Inf. Sci. Technol.*, 59(2), 307–317. DOI: 10.1002/asi.20752 Cited on page(s) 18

Bates, M. J. (1989) The design of browsing and berrypicking techniques for the online search interface. *Online Review*, 13, 407–424. DOI: 10.1108/eb024320 Cited on page(s) 85

Bates, M. J. (2002) Toward an integrated model of information seeking and searching. *Keynote. The 4th Conference on Information Needs, Seeking and Use in Different Contexts*. Lisbon, Portugal. Cited on page(s) 14

Bauerlein, M. (2008) *The Dumbest Generation: How the Digital Age Stupefies Young Americans and Jeopardizes Our Future* (1st ed.). Tarcher. Cited on page(s) 84

Belkin, N. J., Knorz, G., Krause, J., and Womser-Hacker, C. (1993) Interaction with texts: Information retrieval as information-seeking behaviour. *Information Retrieval '93: von der Modellierung zur Anwendung (First Conference of the Gesellschaft fur Informatik Fachgruppe Information Retrieval)* (pp. 55–66). Konstanz, Germany: Universitaetsverlag Konstanz. Cited on page(s) 7

Bell, G. (2001) A personal digital store. *Communications of the ACM*, 44(1), 86–91. Retrieved from http://portal.acm.org/citation.cfm?doid=357489.357513 DOI: 10.1145/357489.357513 Cited on page(s) 41

Bell, Gordon, Gemmell, J., and Lueder, R. (2004) Challenges in using lifetime personal information stores. *Proceedings of the 27th annual international ACM SIGIR conference on Research and development in information retrieval* (pp. 1–1). Sheffield, United Kingdom: ACM. DOI: 10.1145/1008992.1008993 Cited on page(s) 41

Bell, G. and Gemmell, J. (2009) *Total Recall: How the E-Memory Revolution Will Change Everything*. Dutton, New York. Cited on page(s) 41

Bergman, M. K. (2001) The Deep Web: Surfacing Hidden Value. *Journal of Electronic Publishing*, 7(1), 1–17. DOI: 10.3998/3336451.0007.104 Cited on page(s) 85

Bergman, Ofer, Beyth-Marom, R., and Nachmias, R. (2006) The project fragmentation problem in personal information management. *Proceedings of the SIGCHI conference on Human Factors in computing systems* (pp. 271–274). Montreal, Quebec, Canada: ACM. DOI: 10.1145/1124772.1124813 Cited on page(s) 11

Bergman, O., Boardman, R., Gwizdka, J., and Jones, W. (2004) A special interest group session on personal information management. CHI '04 extended abstracts on Human factors in computing systems. Cited on page(s) 13

Bergman, Ofer, Whittaker, S., Sanderson, M., Nachmias, R., and Ramamoorthy, A. (2010) The effect of folder structure on personal file navigation. *J. Am. Soc. Inf. Sci. Technol.*, 61(12), 2426– 2441. DOI: 10.1002/asi.21415 Cited on page(s) 10

Bergman, Ofer, Beyth-Marom, R., Nachmias, R., Gradovitch, N., and Whittaker, S. (2008) Improved search engines and navigation preference in personal information management. *ACM Trans. Inf. Syst.*, 26(4), 1–24. DOI: 10.1145/1402256.1402259 Cited on page(s) 18

Blair, A. (2003) Reading Strategies for Coping With Information Overload ca.1550–1700. *Journal of the History of Ideas*, 64(1), 11-28. DOI: 10.2307/3654293 Cited on page(s) 84

Blair, D. C. and Maron, M. E. (1985) An evaluation of retrieval effectiveness for a full-text document-retrieval system. *Communications of the ACM*, 28(3), 289–299. DOI: 10.1145/3166.3197 Cited on page(s) 85

Boardman, R. and Sasse, M. A. (2004) "Stuff goes into the computer and doesn't come out" A cross-tool study of personal information management. *ACM SIGCHI Conference on Human Factors in Computing Systems (CHI 2004)*. Vienna, Austria. DOI: 10.1145/985692.985766 Cited on page(s) 6, 11, 25

Bradner, E. (2001) Social affordances of computer-mediated communication technology: understanding adoption. *CHI '01 extended abstracts on Human factors in computing systems* (pp. 67–68). Seattle, Washington: ACM. DOI: 10.1145/634067.634111 Cited on page(s) 35

Braman, S. (1989) Defining Information. *Telecommunications Policy*, 13, 233–242. DOI: 10.1016/0308-5961(89)90006-2 Cited on page(s) 1

Brin, D. (1999) *The transparent society: will technology force us to choose between privacy and freedom?* New York: Basic Books. Cited on page(s) 40

Broadbent, D. E. (1958) *Perception and communication*. London, U.K.: Pergamon Press. DOI: 10.1037/10037-000 Cited on page(s) 1

Bruce, H. (2005) Personal, anticipated information need. *Information Research*, 10(3). Retrieved from http://informationr.net/ir/10--3/paper232.html Cited on page(s) 10

Buckland, M. K. (1991) Information as thing. *Journal of the American Society for Information Science*, 42, 351–360. DOI: 10.1002/(SICI)1097-4571(199112)42:10%3C758::AID-ASI12%3E3.0.CO;2-1 Cited on page(s) 1, 21

Buckland, M. K. (1997) What is a document. *Journal of the American Society of Information Science*, 48(9), 804–809. DOI: 10.1002/(SICI)1097-4571(199709)48:9%3C804::AID-ASI5%3E3.0.CO;2-V Cited on page(s) 1, 44

Bush, V. (1945) As We May Think. *The Atlantic Monthly*, 176(1), 641–649. Retrieved from http://www.theatlantic.com/doc/194507/bush DOI: 10.1145/227181.227186 Cited on page(s)

Calore, Michael. (2010), August 17). How Do Native Apps and Web Apps Compare? | Webmonkey | Wired.com.

Retrieved March 23, 2011, from http://www.webmonkey.com/2010/08/howdo-native-apps-and-web-apps-compare/ Cited on page(s) 63

Capurro, R. and Hjørland, B. (2003) The concept of information. *Annual Review of Information Science and Technology (ARIST)* (pp. 343–411). Cited on page(s) 1

Card, S. K., Moran, T. P., and Newell, A. (1983) *The psychology of human-computer interaction*. Hillsdale, NJ: Lawrence Erlbaum Associates. Cited on page(s) 9, 12

Carmody, S., Gross, W., Nelson, T., Rice, D., and Van Dam, A. (1969) A hypertext editing system for the /360. *Pertinent concepts in computer graphics* (pp. 291–330). Urbana, IL: University of Illinois Press. Cited on page(s) 12

Carr, N. (2008) August. Is Google Making Us Stupid? *The Atlantic*. Retrieved from http://www.theatlantic.com/magazine/archive/2008/07/is-google-making-us-stupid/6868/ Cited on page(s) 84

Carrier, L. M. et al. (2009) Multitasking across generations: Multitasking choices and difficulty ratings in three generations of Americans. *Computers in Human Behavior*, 25, 483–489. DOI: 10.1016/j.chb.2008.10.012 Cited on page(s) 50, 52

Carroll, J. M. and Kellogg, W. A. (1989) Artifact as theory-nexus: hermeneutics meets theory-based design. *SIGCHI Bull.*, 20(SI), 7–14. DOI: 10.1145/67450.67452 Cited on page(s) 35

Chi, E. H. (2009) Information Seeking Can Be Social. *Computer*, 42(3), 42–46. doi:10.1109/MC.2009.87 DOI: 10.1109/MC.2009.87 Cited on page(s) 86

Church, K. and Smyth, B. (2008) Understanding mobile information needs. *Proceedings of the 10th international conference on Human computer interaction with mobile devices and services* (pp. 493– 494). Amsterdam, The Netherlands: ACM. DOI: 10.1145/1409240.1409325 Cited on page(s) 37

Civan, Andrea, Jones, W., Klasnja, P., and Bruce, H. (2008) Better to Organize Personal Information by Folders Or by Tags?: The Devil Is in the Details. *68th Annual Meeting of the American Society for Information Science and Technology (ASIST 2008).* Columbus, OH. DOI: 10.1002/meet.2008.1450450214 Cited on page(s) 72

Consolvo, S., McDonald, D. W., and Landay, J. A. (2009) Theory-driven design strategies for technologies that support behavior change in everyday life. *Proceedings of the 27th international conference on Human factors in computing systems* (pp. 405–414). Boston, MA, USA: ACM. DOI: 10.1145/1518701.1518766 Cited on page(s) 48

Consolvo, S., McDonald, D. W., Toscos, T., Chen, M. Y., Froehlich, J., Harrison, B., Klasnja, P., et al. (2008) Activity sensing in the wild: a field trial of ubifit garden. *Proceeding of the twenty-sixth annual SIGCHI conference on Human factors in computing systems* (pp. 1797–1806). Florence, Italy: ACM. DOI: 10.1145/1357054.1357335 Cited on page(s) 48

Cormode, G. and Krishnamurthy, B. (2008) Key differences between Web 1.0 and Web 2.0. 2008. web 2.0. Retrieved from http://firstmonday.org/htbin/cgiwrap/bin/ojs/index.php/fm/article/view/2125/1972 Cited on page(s) 59

Cornelius, I. (2002) Theorizing information. *Annual Review of Information Science and Technology*, 36, 393–425. Cited on page(s) 1

Coughlin (2007). "Tracking himself, so the FBI won't have to," Digital Life with the Star Ledger, 28th October 2007. Cited on page(s) 41

Cutrell, Edward, Czerwinski, M., and Horvitz, E. (2001) Notification, disruption and memory: Effects of messaging interruptions on memory and performance. *Proceedings of Human-Computer Interaction – Interact '01* (pp. 263–269). Tokyo, Japan: IOS Press. Retrieved from http://research.microsoft.com/~cutrell/interact2001messaging.pdf Cited on page(s) 51

Czerwinski, M. and Horvitz, E. (2002) Investigation of Memory for Daily Computing Event. *HCI*. Cited on page(s) 43

Czerwinski, M., Gage, D., Gemmel, J., Marshall, C. C., Perez-Quinones, M., Skeels, M. M., and Catarci, T. (2006) Digital memories in an era of ubiquitous computing and abundant storage. *Communications of the ACM, Special Issue on Personal Information Management*, 49(1), 44–50. DOI: 10.1145/1107458.1107489 Cited on page(s) 41

Czerwinski, Mary, Horvitz, E., and Wilhite, S. (2004) A diary study of task switching and interruptions. *Proceedings of the SIGCHI conference on Human factors in computing systems* (pp. 175–182). Vienna, Austria: ACM. DOI: 10.1145/985692.985715 Cited on page(s) 49, 51

Dabbish, L., Mark, G.,and González, V.M.(2011) Why do i keep interrupting myself?: environment, habit and self-interruption. *Proceedings of the 2011 annual conference on Human factors in computing systems* (pp. 3127–3130). Vancouver, BC, Canada: ACM. DOI: 10.1145/1978942.1979405 Cited on page(s) 48

Dumais, S., Cutrell, E., Cadiz, J., Jancke, G., Sarin, R., and Robbins, D. (2003) Stuff I've seen: a system for personal information retrieval and re-use. *SIGIR 2003: 26th Annual International ACM SIGIR Conference on Research and Development in Information Retrieval* (pp. 72 - 79). Toronto, Canada. DOI: 10.1145/860435.860451 Cited on page(s) 73

Eisenberg, M., Lowe, C. A., and Spitzer, K. L. (2004) *Information literacy?: Essential skills for the information age* (Vol. 2). Westport, CT.: Libraries Unlimited. Cited on page(s) 5

Engelbart, D. (1962) Augmenting human intellect: A conceptual framework. *SRI Report*. Retrieved from http://www.histech.rwth-aachen.de/www/quellen/engelbart/ahi62index.html. Cited on page(s) 12

Engelbart, D. C. (1963) A conceptual framework for the augmentation of man's intellect. *Vistas in information handling*. London: VI Spartan Books. Cited on page(s) 12

Espinoza, F., Persson, P., Sandin, A., Nyström, H., Cacciatore, E., and Bylund, M. (2001) GeoNotes: Social and Navigational Aspects of Location-Based Information Systems. *Proceedings of the 3rd international conference on Ubiquitous Computing* (pp. 2–17). Atlanta, Georgia, USA: Springer-Verlag. Cited on page(s) 37

Fertig, S., Freeman, E., and Gelernter, D. (1996) Lifestreams: an alternative to the desktop metaphor. *Conference on Human Factors in Computing Systems (CHI 1996)* (pp. 410–411). Vancouver, B.C.: ACM. DOI: 10.1145/257089.257404 Cited on page(s) 43

Fidel, R. and Pejtersen, A. M. (2004) From information behaviour research to the design of information systems:

the Cognitive Work Analysis framework. *Information Research*, 10(1). Retrieved from http://informationr.net/ir/10--1/paper210.html Cited on page(s) 7

Freeman, E. and Gelernter, D. (1996) Lifestreams: A storage model for personal data. *ACM SIGMOD Record (ACM Special Interest Group on Management of Data)*, 25(1), 80–86. DOI: 10.1145/381854.381893 Cited on page(s) 43

Furnas, G. W. (1986) Generalized fisheye views. *SIGCHI Bull.*, 17(4), 16–23. doi:10.1145/22339.22342 DOI: 10.1145/22339.22342 Cited on page(s) 75

Gaver, W. (1996) Affordances for interaction: The social is material for design. *Ecological Psychology*, 8(2), 111–129. DOI: 10.1207/s15326969eco0802_2 Cited on page(s) 35

Gaver, W. W. (1991) Technology affordances. *Proceedings of the SIGCHI conference on Human factors in computing systems: Reaching through technology* (pp. 79–84). New Orleans, Louisiana, United States: ACM. DOI: 10.1145/108844.108856 Cited on page(s) 35

Gemmell, J., Bell, G., and Lueder, R. (2006) MyLifeBits: a personal database for everything. *Commun. ACM*, 49(1), 88–95. doi:http//doi.acm.org/10.1145/1107458.1107460 DOI: 10.1145/1107458.1107460 Cited on page(s) 41

Gemmell, J., Bell, G., Lueder, R., Drucker, S., and Wong, C. (2002) Mylifebits: fulfilling the memex vision. *2002 ACM workshops on Multimedia* (pp. 235–238). Juan-les-Pins, France: ACM Press. DOI: 10.1145/641007.641053 Cited on page(s) 41

Gemmell, J., Lueder, R., and Bell, G. (2003) The MyLifeBits lifetime store. *ACM SIGMM 2003 Workshop on Experiential*

Telepresence (ETP 2003) (pp. 80–83). Berkeley, CA. DOI: 10.1145/982484.982500 Cited on page(s) 41

Gillie, T. and Broadbent, D. (1989) What makes interruptions disruptive? A study of length, similarity, and complexity. *Psychological Research*, 50(4), 243–250. DOI: 10.1007/BF00309260 Cited on page(s) 51

Gollwitzer, P. M., and Sheeran, P. (2006) Implementation Intentions and Goal Achievement: A Meta-analysis of Effects and Processes. *Advances in Experimental Social Psychology* (Vol. 38, pp. 69–119). Academic Press. Retrieved from http://www.sciencedirect.com/science/article/pii/S0065260 106380021 DOI: 10.1016/S0065-2601(06)38002-1 Cited on page(s) 89

González, V. M., and Mark, G. (2004) Constant, constant, multitasking craziness': managing multiple working spheres. *CHI 2004* (pp. 113–120). DOI: 10.1145/985692.985707 Cited on page(s) 49

Graham, P. (2001) The Other Road Ahead. Retrieved August 22, 2010, from http://www.paulgraham.com/road.html Cited on page(s) 62

Grudin, J. (1993) Interface: An evolving concept. *Communications of the ACM*, 36(1), 103–111. DOI: 10.1145/255950.153585 Cited on page(s) 9

Grudin, J. (2011) Kai: how media affects learning. *interactions*, 18(5), 70–73. DOI: 10.1145/2008176.2008192 Cited on page(s) 84

Gwizdka, J. and Chignell, M. (2007) Individual Differences. *Personal Information Management:* Seattle, WA: University of Washington Press. Cited on page(s) 6

Hafner, K. (2004) Even Digital Memories Can Fade. *New York Times*. Cited on page(s) 42

Halasz, F. G. (1988) Reflections on NoteCards: seven issues for the next generation of hypermedia systems. *Communications of the ACM*, 31(7), 836–852. DOI: 10.1145/48511.48514 Cited on page(s) 91

Halasz, F. G., Moran, T. P., and Trigg, R. H. (1987) Notecards in a nutshell. *Proceedings of the SIGCHI/GI conference on Human factors in computing systems and graphics interface* (pp. 45–52). Toronto, Ontario, Canada: ACM Press. DOI: 10.1145/29933.30859 Cited on page(s) 91

Hansen, Evan. (2010), August 17. How the Web Wins | Epicenter | Wired.com. *Wired Magazine*. Retrieved March 23, 2011, from http://www.wired.com/epicenter/2010/08/how-theweb-wins/ Cited on page(s) 55

Head, A. J. and Eisenberg, M. (2010) How today's college students use Wikipedia for course-related research. *First Monday*, 15(3). Retrieved from http://firstmonday.org/htbin/cgiwrap/bin/ojs/index.php/fm/article/view/2830/2476 Cited on page(s) 84

Holt, J. (2011), March 3. Smarter, Happier, More Productive. *London Review of Books*, pp. 9–12. Retrieved from http://www.lrb.co.uk/v33/n05/jim-holt/smarter-happier-more-productive Cited on page(s) 84

Hsu, J. (2008), September 18. The Secrets of Storytelling: Why We Love a Good Yarn: Scientific American. *Scientific American Mind*. Retrieved January 22, 2012, from http://www.scientificamerican.com/article.cfm?id=the-secrets-of-storytellingi# comments Cited on page(s) 90

Iqbal, S. T. and Horvitz, E. (2007) Disruption and recovery of computing tasks: field study, analysis, and directions. *Proceedings of the SIGCHI conference on Human factors in computing systems* (pp. 677– 686). San Jose, California, USA: ACM. DOI: 10.1145/1240624.1240730 Cited on page(s) 49

Jin, J. and Dabbish, L. A. (2009) Self-interruption on the computer: a typology of discretionary task interleaving. *Proceedings of the 27th international conference on Human factors in computing systems* (pp. 1799–1808). Boston, MA, USA: ACM. DOI: 10.1145/1518701.1518979 Cited on page(s) 48

Jokela, T., Lehikoinen, J. T., and Korhonen, H. (2008) Mobile multimedia presentation editor: enabling creation of audio-visual stories on mobile devices. *Proceeding of the twenty-sixth annual SIGCHI conference on Human factors in computing systems* (pp. 63–72). Florence, Italy: ACM. DOI: 10.1145/1357054.1357066 Cited on page(s) 38

Jones, W. (1986a) The memory extender personal filing system. Proceedings of the SIGCHI conference on Human factors in computing systems. DOI: 10.1145/22339.22387 Cited on page(s) 41

Jones, W. (1986b) On the applied use of human memory models: The Memory Extender personal filing system. *International Journal of Man Machine Studies*, 25, 191– 228. DOI: 10.1016/S0020-7373(86)80076-1 Cited on page(s) 41

Jones, W. (1988) "As we may think"?: Psychological considerations in the design of a personal filing system. *Cognitive science and its application for human/computer interaction*. Hillsdale, NJ: Lawrence Erlbaum. Cited on page(s) 41

Jones, W. (2004) Finders, keepers? The present and future perfect in support of personal information management. *First* *Monday,* http://www.firstmonday.dk/issues/issue9_3/jones/index.html. DOI: 10.1002/meet.1450420151 Cited on page(s) 6, 29

Jones, W. (2007) *Keeping Found Things Found: The Study and Practice of Personal Information Management.* San Francisco, CA: Morgan Kaufmann Publishers. Cited on page(s) 3, 22, 25, 27, 39

Jones, W. and Teevan, J. (2007). Personal Information Management. Seattle, WA: University of Washingon Press. Cited on page(s) 13

Jones, W. and Ross, B. (2006) Human cognition and personal information management. *Handbook of applied cognition.* Cited on page(s) 6

Jones, W., Bruce, H., and Dumais, S. (2003) How do people get back to information on the web? How can they do it better? *9th IFIP TC13 International Conference on Human-Computer Interaction (INTERACT 2003).* Zurich, Switzerland. Cited on page(s) 42

Jones, W., Dumais, S., and Bruce, H. (2002) Once found, what then??: A study of "keeping" behaviors in the personal use of web information. Presented at the 65th Annual Meeting of the American Society for Information Science and Technology (ASIST 2002), Philadelphia, PA. Cited on page(s) 10

Jones, W. and Maier, D. (2003). Report from the session on personal information management. Workshop of the information and data management program. Seattle, WA: National Science Foundation Information. Retrieved from http://kftf.ischool.washington.edu/docs/Summary_of_PIM2 003.pdf. Cited on page(s) 3

Jones, W., Phuwanartnurak, A. J., Gill, R., and Bruce, H. (2005) Don't take my folders away! Organizing personal information to get things done. *ACM SIGCHI Conference on Human Factors in Computing Systems (CHI 2005)* (Vol. 2005, pp. 1505–1508). Portland, OR: ACM Press. DOI: 10.1145/1056808.1056952 Cited on page(s) 6, 10, 11

Jones, W. (2010) No knowledge but through information. *First Monday*, 15(9). Retrieved from http://firstmonday.org/htbin/cgiwrap/bin/ojs/index.php/fm/article/viewArticle/3062/2600 Cited on page(s) 56

Jones, W. (2011) XooML: XML in support of many tools working on a single organization of personal information. *Proceedings of the 2011 iConference* (pp. 478–488). Seattle, Washington: ACM. Retrieved from http://delivery.acm.org/10.1145/1950000/1940827/p478-jones.pdf?key1=1940827andkey2=5397719921andcoll=DLanddl=ACMandip=205.175.115.100andCFID=11076833andCFTOKEN=71585935 DOI: 10.1145/1940761.1940827 Cited on page(s) 45, 79

Jones, W. and Anderson, K. M. (2011) Many Vews, Many Modes, Many Tools... One Structure: Towards a Non-disruptive Integration of Personal Information. *Proceedings of the 22nd ACM conference on Hypertext and hypermedia* (pp. 113–122). Eindhoven, The Netherlands: ACM. DOI: 10.1145/1995966.1995984 Cited on page(s) 45, 79, 81

Jones, W., Hou, D., Sethanandha, B. D., Bi, S., and Gemmell, J. (2010) Planz to put our digital information in its place. *Proceedings of the 28th of the international conference extended abstracts on Human factors in computing systems* (pp. 2803–2812). Atlanta, Georgia, USA: ACM. DOI: 10.1145/1753846.1753866 Cited on page(s) 80, 89

Kalnikaité, V. and Whittaker, S. (2007) Software or wetware?: discovering when and why people use digital prosthetic memory. *Proceedings of the SIGCHI conference on Human factors in computing systems* (pp. 71–80). San Jose, California, USA: ACM. DOI: 10.1145/1240624.1240635 Cited on page(s) 41, 43

Kalnikaité, V. and Whittaker, S. (2008) Cueing digital memory: how and why do digital notes help us remember? *Proceedings of the 22nd British HCI Group Annual Conference on HCI 2008: People and Computers XXII: Culture, Creativity, Interaction - Volume 1* (pp. 153–161). Liverpool, United Kingdom: British Computer Society. Cited on page(s) 41

Kane, S. K., Avrahami, D., Wobbrock, J. O., Harrison, B., Rea, A. D., Philipose, M., and LaMarca, A. (2009) Bonfire: a nomadic system for hybrid laptop-tabletop interaction. *Proceedings of the 22nd annual ACM symposium on User interface software and technology* (pp. 129–138). Victoria, BC, Canada: ACM. DOI: 10.1145/1622176.1622202 Cited on page(s) 39

Kaplan, A. M. and Haenlein, M. (2009a) Consumer Use and Business Potential of Virtual Worlds: The Case of "Second Life." *International Journal on Media Management*, 11(3–4), 93-101. DOI: 10.1080/14241270903047008 Cited on page(s) 86

Kaplan, A. M. and Haenlein, M. (2009b) The fairyland of Second Life: Virtual social worlds and how to use them. *Business Horizons*, 52(6), 563–572. DOI: 10.1016/j.bushor.2009.07.002 Cited on page(s) 86

Karger, D. R. and Quan, D. (2004). Collections: flexible, essential tools for information management. *ACM SIGCHI Conference on Human factors in Computing Systems, Extended Abstracts (CHI 2004).* Cited on page(s) 25

Klasnja, P., Consolvo, S., Jung, J., Greenstein, B. M., LeGrand, L., Powledge, P., and Wetherall, D. (2009) "When I am on Wi-Fi, I am fearless": privacy concerns and practices in everyday Wi-Fi use. *Proceedings of the 27th international conference on Human factors in computing systems* (pp. 1993–2002). Boston, MA, USA: ACM. DOI: 10.1145/1518701.1519004 Cited on page(s) 40

Lansdale, M. (1988) The psychology of personal information management. *Appl. Ergon.*, 19(1), 55–66. DOI: 10.1016/0003-6870(88)90199-8 Cited on page(s) 12

Lansdale, M. and Edmonds, E. (1992) Using memory for events in the design of personal filing systems. *International Journal of Man-Machine Studies*, 36, 97–126. DOI: 10.1016/0020-7373(92)90054-O Cited on page(s) 43

Licklider, J. C. R. (1960) Man-computer symbiosis. *IRE Transactions on Human Factors in Electronics, HFE-1*, 4–11. DOI: 10.1109/THFE2.1960.4503259 Cited on page(s)

Lillie, Rhonda. (2009), October 25). Second Life Blogs. Retrieved March 23, 2011, from http://www.slprofiles.com/secondlifeblog.asp?u=11649 Cited on page(s) 86

Loftus, E. (1993) The reality of repressed memories. *American Psychologist*, 48(5), 518–537. DOI: 10.1037/0003-066X.48.5.518 Cited on page(s) 42

Ludford, P. J., Frankowski, D., Reily, K., Wilms, K., and Terveen, L. (2006) Because I carry my cell phone anyway: functional location-based reminder applications.

Proceedings of the SIGCHI conference on Human Factors in computing systems (pp. 889–898). Montréal, Québec, Canada: ACM. DOI: 10.1145/1124772.1124903 Cited on page(s) 37, 54

Lutters, W. G., Ackerman, M. S., and Zhou, X. (2007) Group Information Management. *Personal Information Management: Challenges and Opportunities.* Seattle, WA: University of Washington Press. Cited on page(s) 4

Machlup, F. (1983) Semantic Quirks in Studies of Information. *The Study of Information: Interdisciplinary Messages.* (pp. 641–671). New York: Wiley. Cited on page(s) 1

MacLean, A., Young, R. M., and Moran, T. P. (1989) Design rationale: the argument behind the artifact. *SIGCHI Bull.,* 20(SI), 247–252. DOI: 10.1145/67450.67497 Cited on page(s) 35

Malone, T. W. (1983) How do people organize their desks: implications for the design of office information-systems. *ACM Transactions on Office Information Systems*, 1(1), 99–112. Retrieved from http://doi.acm.org/10.1145/357423.357430 DOI: 10.1145/357423.357430 Cited on page(s) 6

Mann, S. and Niedzviecki, H. (2001) *Cyborg: Digital destiny and human possibility in the age of the wearable computer.* Toronto: Doubleday Canada. Cited on page(s) 41

Mann, S., Sehgal, A., and Fung, J. (2004) Continuous lifelong capture of personal experience using eyetap. *First ACM Workshop on Continuous Archival and Retrieval of Personal Experiences (CARPE '04)* (pp. 1–21.). New York, NY, USA. DOI: 10.1145/1026653.1026654 Cited on page(s) 41

Marchionini, G. (2006) Exploratory search: from finding to understanding. *Communications of the ACM*, 49(4), 41–46. DOI: 10.1145/1121949.1121979 Cited on page(s) 85

Mark, G., González, V. M., and Harris, J. (2005) No task left behind?: examining the nature of fragmented work. *CHI 2005* (pp. 321–330). Portland, OR. DOI: 10.1145/1054972.1055017 Cited on page(s) 49

Mark, Gloria, Gudith, D., and Klocke, U. (2008) The cost of interrupted work: more speed and stress. *Proceeding of the twenty-sixth annual SIGCHI conference on Human factors in computing systems* (pp. 107–110). Florence, Italy: ACM. DOI: 10.1145/1357054.1357072 Cited on page(s) 49, 51

Marshall, C. C. (2009) No bull, no spin: a comparison of tags with other forms of user metadata. *Proceedings of the 9th ACM/IEEE-CS joint conference on Digital libraries* (pp. 241–250). Austin, TX, USA: ACM. DOI: 10.1145/1555400.1555438 Cited on page(s) 90

Naisbitt, J. (1984) *Megatrends: Ten new directions transforming our lives.* New York: Warner. Cited on page(s)

Naumer and Fisher (2010) "Information Needs," *Encyclopedia of Library and Information Sciences,* Third Edition, 1:1, 2452–2458. Cited on page(s) 27

Neisser, U. (1967) *Cognitive psychology.* New York: Appleton-Century Crofts. Cited on page(s)

Nelson, T. H. (1965) File structure for the complex, the changing, and the indeterminate. *Proceedings of the 1965 20th ACM/CSC-ER national conference* (pp. 84–100). Cleveland, OH: ACM. DOI: 10.1145/800197.806036 Cited on page(s) 12

Nelson, T. H. (1982) *Literary machines*. Sausalito, CA: Mindful Press. Cited on page(s) 12, 91

Newell, A. and Simon, H. A. (1972) *Human problem solving*. Englewood Cliffs, NJ: Prentice-Hall. Cited on page(s) 12

Newell, A., Shaw, J. C., and Simon, H. (1958) Elements of a theory of human problem solving. *Psychological Review*, 65, 151–166. DOI: 10.1037/h0048495 Cited on page(s) 12

Norman, D. A. (1988) *The psychology of everyday things*. New York: Basic Books. Cited on page(s) 12, 35

Nürnberg, P. J., Leggett, J. J., Schneider, E. R., and Schnase, J. L. (1996) Hypermedia operating systems: a new paradigm for computing. *Proceedings of the the seventh ACM conference on Hypertext* (pp. 194–202). Bethesda, Maryland, United States: ACM. DOI: 10.1145/234828.234847 Cited on page(s) 81

O'Hara and Shadbolt (2008). *The spy in the coffee machine: the end of privacy as we know it*. Oxford. Cited on page(s) 40

O'Hara et al. (2008). Lifelogging: Privacy and empowerment with memories for life, *Identity in the Information Society*, Volume 1, Number 1, 155-172, DOI: DOI: 10.1007/s12394-009-0008-4. Cited on page(s) 41

Ong, W. J. (2007) *Orality and Literacy: The Technologizing of the Word* (2nd cd.). Taylor and Francis. Cited on page(s) 91

Ophir, E., Nass, C., and Wagner, A. (2009) Cognitive control in media multitaskers. *PNAS*, 106(37), 15583–15587. Retrieved from http://www.pnas.org/content/106/37/15583.abstract DOI: 10.1073/pnas.0903620106 Cited on page(s) 50

Papert, S. (1993) Obsolete Skill Set: The 3 Rs. *Obsolete Skill Set: The 3 Rs — Literacy and Letteracy in the Media Ages*. Retrieved January 21, 2012, from http://www.papert.org/articles/ObsoleteSkillSet.html Cited on page(s) 59

Pashler, H. (1994) Dual-Task Interference in Simple Tasks: Data and Theory. *Psychological Bulletin*, 116(2), 220–244. DOI: 10.1037/0033-2909.116.2.220 Cited on page(s) 50

Pirolli, P. and Card, S. (1999) Information foraging. *Psychological Review*, 106(4), 643–675. DOI: 10.1037/0033-295X.106.4.643 Cited on page(s) 13

Pratt, W., Unruh, K., Civan, A., and Skeels, M. (2006) Personal health information management. *Communications of the ACM*, 49(1), 51–55. DOI: 10.1145/1107458.1107490 Cited on page(s) 5

Rist, Oliver. (2006), October 2). Can Web-based applications outwit, outplay, outlast the desktop? | Applications - InfoWorld. *InfoWorld*. Retrieved March 23, 2011, from http://www.infoworld.com/t/applications/can-web-based-applications-outwit-outplay-outlast-desktop-122?page=0,6 Cited on page(s) 63

Salvucci, D. D., Taatgen, N. A., and Borst, J. P. (2009) Toward a unified theory of the multitasking continuum: from concurrent performance to task switching, interruption, and resumption. *Proceedings of the 27th international conference on Human factors in computing systems* (pp. 1819–1828). Boston, MA, USA: ACM. DOI: 10.1145/1518701.1518981 Cited on page(s) 49

Seifert, C. M. and Patalano, A. L. (2001) Opportunism in memory: Preparing for chance encounters. *Current Directions in Psychological Science*, 10(6), 198–201. DOI: 10.1111/1467-8721.00148 Cited on page(s) 89

Sellen, A. J. and Whittaker, S. (2010) Beyond total capture: a constructive critique of lifelogging. *Commun. ACM*, 53(5), 70–77. DOI: 10.1145/1735223.1735243 Cited on page(s) 41, 42, 84

Sellen, A. J., Fogg, A., Aitken, M., Hodges, S., Rother, C., and Wood, K. (2007) Do life-logging technologies support memory for the past?: an experimental study using sensecam. *Proceedings of the SIGCHI conference on Human factors in computing systems* (pp. 81–90). San Jose, California, USA: ACM. DOI: 10.1145/1240624.1240636 Cited on page(s) 41, 42

Shannon, C. E. (1948) A mathematical theory of communication. *The Bell System Technical Journal*, 27, 379–423, 623–656. DOI: 10.1145/584091.584093 Cited on page(s) 1, 12

Shannon, C. E. and Weaver, W. (1949) *The Mathematical Theory of Communication*. Urbana, IL: University of Illinois Press. Cited on page(s) 1, 12

Sheeran, P., Webb, T. L., and Gollwitzer, P. M. (2005) The Interplay Between Goal Intentions and Implementation Intentions. *Personality and Social Psychology Bulletin*, 31(1), 87–98. DOI: 10.1177/0146167204271308 Cited on page(s) 89

Simon, H. A. (1969) *The sciences of the artificial.* Cambridge, MA: MIT Press. Cited on page(s) 51

Simon, H. A. and Newell, A. (1958) Heuristic problem solving: The next advance in operations research. *Operations Research*, 6, 1–10. DOI: 10.1287/opre.6.1.1 Cited on page(s) 12

Sparrow, B., Liu, J., and Wegner, D. M. (2011) Google Effects on Memory: Cognitive Consequences of Having

Information at Our Fingertips. *Science*, 333(6043), 776–778. DOI: 10.1126/science.1207745 Cited on page(s) 85

Teevan, J., Alvarado, C., Ackerman, M. S., and Karger, D. R. (2004) The perfect search engine Is not enough: A study of orienteering behavior in directed search. *ACM SIGCHI Conference on Human Factors in Computing Systems (CHI 2004)* (pp. 415–422). Vienna, Austria. DOI: 10.1145/985692.985745 Cited on page(s) 18

Teevan, Jaime, Liebling, D. J., and Ravichandran Geetha, G. (2011) Understanding and predicting personal navigation. *Proceedings of the fourth ACM international conference on Web search and data mining*, WSDM '11 (pp. 85–94). New York, NY, USA: ACM. DOI: 10.1145/1935826.1935848 Cited on page(s) 85

Turner, M., Budgen, D., and Brereton, P. (2003) Turning Software into a Service. *Computer*, 36(10), 38–44. DOI: 10.1109/MC.2003.1236470 Cited on page(s) 62

Van House, N., Davis, M., Ames, M., Finn, M., and Viswanathan, V. (2005) The uses of personal networked digital imaging: an empirical study of cameraphone photos and sharing. *CHI '05 extended abstracts on Human factors in computing systems* (pp. 1853–1856). Portland, OR, USA: ACM. DOI: 10.1145/1056808.1057039 Cited on page(s) 36, 38

Volz, J., Bizer, C., Gaedke, M., and Kobilarov, G. (2009) Discovering and Maintaining Links on the

Web of Data. *Proceedings of the 8th International Semantic Web Conference* (pp. 650–665). Chantilly, VA: Springer-Verlag. DOI: 10.1007/978-3-642-04930-9_41 Cited on page(s) 58

Weinreich, H., Obendorf, H., Herder, E., and Mayer, M. (2008) Not quite the average: An empirical study of Web use. *ACM Trans. Web*, 2(1), 1–31. DOI: 10.1145/1326561.1326566 Cited on page(s) 63

Weitzner, D. (2007) Whose Name is it Anyway? Decentralized Identity Systems on the Web. *IEEE Internet Computer Technology and Society column*. DOI: 10.1109/MIC.2007.95 Cited on page(s) 44, 87

Whitlaker, S. and Sidner, C. (1996) Email overload: exploring personal information management of email. CHI 1996: ACM SIGCHI Conference on Human Factors in Computing Systems. Retrieved from http://www.acm.org/sigchi/chi96/proceedings/papers/Whittaker/sw_txt.htm DOI: 10.1145/238386.238530 Cited on page(s) 6, 9, 10

Whittaker, Steve. (2011) Personal information management: from information consumption to curation. *Annual Review of Information Science and Technology*, 45, 3–62. DOI: 10.1145/238386.238530 Cited on page(s) 15, 16

Whittaker, Steve, Bergman, O., and Clough, P. (2010) Easy on that trigger dad: a study of long term family photo retrieval. *Personal Ubiquitous Comput.*, 14(1), 31–43. DOI: 10.1007/s00779-009-0218-7 Cited on page(s) 6

Yates, F. A. (1966) *The art of memory*. Chicago: University of Chicago Press. Cited on page(s) 11

Yates, J. (1989) *Control through communication: The rise of system in American management*. Baltimore, MD: Johns Hopkins University Press. Cited on page(s) 11

Zins, C. (2007) Conceptual Approaches for Defining Data, Information, and Knowledge. *Journal of the American*

Society for Information Science and Technology, 58(4), 479–493. DOI: 10.1002/asi.20508 Cited on page(s) 1, 56

Author's Biography

WILLIAM JONES

William Jones is a Research Associate Professor in the Information School at the University of Washington where he manages the Keeping Found Things Found group (kftf.ischool.washington.edu). He has published in the areas of personal information management (PIM), human-computer interaction, information retrieval and human cognition. Prof. Jones wrote the book "Keeping Found Things Found: The Study and Practice of Personal Information Management" and also edited the book "Personal Information Management" (with co-editor Jaime Teevan). He holds several patents relating to search and PIM from his work as a program manager at Microsoft in Office and then in MSN Search. Prof. Jones received his doctorate from Carnegie-Mellon University for research into human memory.

Printed in the United States
by Baker & Taylor Publisher Services